ENDOR$

"Some people when they are born (if they are lucky) find out what they are great at and what they are supposed to do the rest of their life. Letitia was fortunate to find that out early. She is the ultimate auctiontainer and should have a tattoo saying, BLOOD FROM A ROCK.

Letitia is glamorous and charismatic. She can read a room of bidders and no one can say no to her. Beneath her glamorous exterior beats a compassionate and generous heart. We, at our nonprofit Solid Rock, can't imagine doing an auction for our golf tournament or annual Alice Cooper's Christmas Pudding charity concert without her at the helm. She is family and she is loved."

—Alice and Sheryl Cooper

"For sure, Letitia is without equal. She's what every auction-eer wants to be—an excellent and exceptionally quick-witted entertainer and one hell of a closer."

—Bob Parsons, Founder of GoDaddy

"With her striking elegance Letitia takes no prisoners...quite simply the most commanding presence in her field. She leaves no heart unturned and no mind in doubt. It is a joy to watch her magic."

—John O'Hurley, Actor

"Letitia Frye is THE BEST auctioneer we've ever encountered. She can turn a low-energy crowd into a high-energy crowd with just a few sentences. She's quick, she's sharp, but most importantly, she has a heart of gold. She's passionate about what she does, and it shows."

—Patrick and Cathy Warburton

LETITIA FRYE

THE AUCTIONTAINER™

NO RESERVE

TAKE OWNERSHIP
AND LIVE **YOUR** LIFE
WITHOUT LIMITATIONS

To my daughter Hunter and my son Duke,
without whom none of this would be possible

Acknowledgments

I would be remiss if I did not take the time to thank a few amazing people who may have actually saved my life, let alone gave me the strength and wherewithal to complete this book.

First and foremost are my children, Hunter and Duke. These two champions have watched their mother fall down and get back up more times than they can count, but they never once gave up on believing in me. For all the countless poems, drawings, handwritten notes of encouragement, and constant companionship, support, and love you gave, you will forever remain my North Star, pointing my soul in the right direction.

To Dr. Mark, for allowing me to call at ridiculous times in the night and early mornings after my accident. For literally talking me off a ledge, listening to me cry, and helping me understand that the effects of my TBI and PTSD would one day pass, even after the shock of having a seizure while alone on the road. Thank you for being my unconventional, all-too-human Doc.

To Kelly and Mike, for giving me the honor of conducting your wedding ceremony, not realizing it would one day lead to the cost of being my attorney after being hit by a car. For countless calls of tears, fears, and impatience while searching for the light at the end of the proverbial tunnel of the destruction of life as I knew it. Thank you for never giving up on me and for fighting for me and my children, at no cost to any of us.

To Karl and Ann, there are no words to describe the hell we endured together or the walk we would take side by side through unspeakable terror, pain, and uncertainty. My love for you both is as deep as any could run. Even if we were not born of the same blood, my heart would not beat if it were not for you two. Thank you for being my family.

To my friends, my tribe, you know who you are. Thank you for coming out to be by my side for the highest highs and the deepest lows of this journey of life. It is as if you are all one being and simply shapeshift into individuals as you take turns showing up on a daily basis, even when you are not asked to do so. It is through you that every breath that dries the ink of this book is possible, because I am only possible through you.

To Rachel for the many late nights dictating my thoughts and words to you while you typed away. For the wall of Post-it Notes piecing the trails of my life into one. For your willingness to dive into the emotion of my grief, to share in the laughter and joy of creation, and to stand in the fire with me, vulnerable and unafraid.

To David Wildasin, thank you for taking a shot with an unknown, first-time author and seeing the brand before the rest of the world would come to do so. For hours of hysterical and mind-expanding conversation and the more-than-occasional stupid humor.

To Jen Janechek, for editing my wild prose and taming that untrained beast. For talking woman to woman, mom to mom, wife to wife before, after, and during our journey together. I see you, and I know you see me.

A special thank you to Mr. Burns and Ms. Schwartz, my middle and high school English teachers, who saw talent in a young writer before she could ever see any kind of talent in herself. For cultivating me as a student and introducing me to my love of literature. Teachers are indeed the unsung heroes of life. Thank you for being mine.

To every person along this path who told me I would never make it. Those in my industry, those in the literary world, the field of entertainment, and those in my family and personal life. To all of you who tried to put out the flame in my heart, I sincerely and honestly thank you. You turned out be the greatest fuel to stoke the flames of my soul and set me free to my highest heights.

Lastly, to Steven. From the moment you came crashing into my young life, sparks literally flying, to the day I would stand over you and watch those sparks go out, you have shaped my life into what it is, for better or worse, and through our children you will continue to do so. You always said we would have the most beautiful babies. Thank you for being my friend, my lover, the father of my children, my greatest cross to bear, and the lesson my life was created to learn. See you on the other side.

"*And the day came* when the risk to remain tight in a bud was more painful than the risk it took to blossom."

—Anaïs Nin

Published and distributed by:

SOUND WISDOM

P.O. Box 310

Shippensburg, PA 17257-0310

717-530-2122

info@soundwisdom.com

www.soundwisdom.com

Cover/jacket designer: Eileen Rockwell

ISBN 13: 978-1-64095-176-1

ISBN 13 eBook: 978-1-64095-177-8

Library of Congress Cataloging-in-Publication Data

Names: Frye, Letitia, author.

Title: No reserve : take ownership and live your life without limitations / Letitia Frye, The Auctiontainer.

Description: Shippensburg, PA : Sound Wisdom, [2020]

Identifiers: LCCN 2019056947 | ISBN 9781640951761 (paperback) | ISBN 9781640951778 (ebook)

Subjects: LCSH: Self-actualization (Psychology) | Happiness.

Classification: LCC BF637.S4 F79 2020 | DDC 158.1--dc23

LC record available at https://lccn.loc.gov/2019056947

For Worldwide Distribution, Printed in the U.S.A.

1 2 3 4 5 6 7 8 / 24 23 22 21 20

CONTENTS

FOREWORD

As a woman in business, a Hall of Fame keynote speaker, and former president of Arbonne with annual sales of over $980 million, I thought I had seen just about everything, especially when it came to attending charity events. And then came Letitia Frye.

The first time I saw Letitia I was not sure if I was watching an auction, a circus act in heels, listening to an outstanding speaker, or maybe a little of each. Either way, it was unlike anything I had ever experienced. Over the years, I watched Letitia as she grew... both her business and her stage presence, eventually becoming what is now known across the country as "The Auctiontainer."

Letitia has the ability to literally transform an audience through her explosive and heartfelt passion.

I have had the pleasure of getting to know Letitia off the stage as much as on, and I can tell you that she is her authentic self no matter where you find her. That is why it did not surprise me that Letitia chose to write a book outlining the path to an authentic and best self, nor did it surprise me that she would title the book with the auction terminology *No Reserve*. You will discover in this book that she is a bit "tongue and cheek" to say the least. Let's just say humor is not lost on this gal, which is a good thing considering how much tragedy she has had to overcome.

Letitia is a brilliant performer who instantly identifies with any audience, but it is the way she approaches life off the stage that may be her BEST performance. In this book she shares not only her successes, but her losses as well, and outlines the methods she uses to continually overcome any obstacle in front of her, while using the experience to become an even better version of herself. And just when I think I have seen her at her best, she comes out with something a cut above the last. How? I have wondered that myself. And thanks to her new book, we are all about to find out exactly what it means to live a life without reserve; to remove limitations, both perceived and real; and to live life out loud and to its fullest potential.

Letitia literally draws a map not only of how she has done it, but how any of us can do it too. In fact, after decades in the speaking business, I was amazed when it took her seconds at lunch to put into simple, clear words something I had been driving at in my own keynotes for years. She was able to articulate that while we are all told it takes only one person to believe in us to change the direction of a life, no one told you that one person is YOU. I told her I would be using that from my own stage and credit her for saying it.

That being said, I should warn you, this gal does not know how to sugarcoat anything, so be prepared to laugh, cry, gasp, and maybe even pee a little. All kidding aside, you are about to enter a new world, one where there are no limitations to what you can achieve, a life of opportunity that you create yourself, a life with NO RESERVE.

—Rita Davenport, CSP, CPAE
award-winning keynote speaker, author,
and past president of Arbonne International

NO RISK, NO REWARD

Only those who will risk going too far can possibly find out how far one can go.

—T. S. Eliot

F rom the podium a voice rings out: "Lot 1!" You lean in to hear what item is for sale, when images from your past, present, and—seemingly—future appear on the screen.

You realize, in an uncanny turn of events, that the people around you are about to start bidding on your life, determining what value to place on it. *What will it go for?* you wonder. You grip the seat, anxiously awaiting to hear the starting bid. *What if it sells for too low of a price?*

You look around. From the looks of the scanty crowd, it appears that you might have set a reserve price at this auction, ensuring your life must reach a minimum value to sell. But the poor attendance has made you question your strategy: *Whom have I excluded by restricting my reach? How will I grow my value if I'm playing it safe? What's holding me back? Why am I not "all in"?*

> How will I grow my value
> if I'm playing it safe?

Life is like an auction: you get your best returns if you don't set a reserve on it. Anyone who wants to live a meaningful, fulfilling, invigorating life that makes an impression on the world must learn to live their life with *no reserve.*

But what does that mean, exactly?

Let's say that there's someone who wants to sell their house for $2 million, yet they really need to move on with their life and follow their new plan. So, they decide to hire an auctioneer. They know that they do not want to take an offer under $1 million for their house. They also are scared that they may not achieve or acquire all that they need in order to succeed in their next step. Consequently, they tell the auctioneer that they would like to set a reserve—or a minimum bid—on the sale of their property for $1 million. The auctioneer tells them that might be one of the worst decisions they could make if they truly would like to garner a high price on the sale of their home. Why would she say that? It's because setting a limitation is tantamount to publicly declaring, "This is as far as I'm willing to go." In other words, "I'm not willing to take a risk." Without risk, there is little chance for great reward.

> Without risk, there is little chance for great reward.

If you listen to the auctioneer, she will tell you to remove the reserve and sell the property absolute, or "no reserve." A no-reserve auction does not have a minimum bid. It can start as low as a dollar. The reason that no-reserve auctions tend to bring in more money is that when there is no perceived limitation, there is room for chance—as in, *unlimited* opportunities for success. The public will come out in far greater numbers to this house sale because they think they've got a good shot at getting a great deal on a $2 million property. The truth is, more bodies in the room in a competitive environment means better odds that the seller will have better results. The bidding will become fast and furious, with the "hammer price," or final sale price, reaching heights unheard of for an auction with reserve.

Many people are risk averse, yet they talk about wanting to be an entrepreneur or desiring to take their company to the "next level." How can you create great things in life without taking any risks? I have made a number of daring moves and bet on myself. Some of the risks were successes, and others were painful lessons—and I do not regret a single one of them. I've lived a life filled with unimaginable tragedy and yet incredible abundance, and my journey has taught me that if you want to live an authentic life, enjoy great success, and make a difference in the world, you have to remove your reserve, step out of your comfort zone, and seize opportunities as they come.

Even my pursuit of becoming a female auctioneer was a risk, because women haven't traditionally been hired as auctioneers by high-profile organizations. I disrupted a male-dominated profession. I had some cheerleaders along the way, but the naysayers outnumbered them five to one. I used a couple of bright stars to navigate by—my passion and my perspective—and so the risks I took were not, in all reality, wild ones; they were calculated. My passion drove me past the limitations and challenges that were already set before me as a woman, a single mother, and a rookie auctioneer. I broke the rules constantly and came out on the other side stronger personally and professionally. You can as well—if you take the reserve off your life and realize that your value is too great to be restricted by minimum bids.

This book will help you stop limiting yourself in all your endeavors—your career, your relationships, and your personal growth. You *can* have everything you want in life, but you have to stop looking for opportunities to come to you or for the road suddenly to become easier. Oftentimes, you have to make your own path: do the work before getting paid for it, create your own network by mentoring others, and give generously of yourself when you think you have little or nothing to offer. As you'll discover in this book, life will present both landmines and roses, but if you add value regardless of whichever phase you're in, then you will never be found wanting. So cast off the reserve you've placed on yourself and start L I V I N G your authentic, *absolute* life.

CHAPTER 1

LIVE YOUR AUTHENTIC STORY

For me, it is far better to grasp the Universe as it really is than to persist in delusion, however satisfying and reassuring.

—Carl Sagan

I f you had met me in 2003, you would have thought that I had quite the life, one for which even Barbie in her dream-house would die. I married my college best friend, we made some beautiful babies, and I lived in a palatial home. I was in the happily ever after of a Cinderella story. I was living a dream life, except that it was someone else's dream. I won't pretend that having money did not have its perks, but it was a self-made prison cell I had created for myself. I was smiling outwardly to the world while silently dying inside. My husband was a "Wolf of Wall Street" in sheep's clothing. The drugs, the parties, and the chaos kept me locked up inside. I had literally become Barbie—eternally smiling my drawn-on smile while being plastic and hollow. It took years of dizzying highs and lows and a number of startling wake-up calls to get me to a place where I could begin to create an authentic life.

Gilding the Cage

I met Steve, the man who would become my husband and father of my children, while I was a freshman at the University of Southern California in 1987. At the time, I was dating a boy named Jeff, who was in the same fraternity as Steve. That did not bother Steve. When he first met me at the fraternity, he declared to me without hesitation: "You are going to be my wife." I thought he was nuts and moved on.

Fast-forward to my sophomore year, when after a double date Jeff got pulled over for driving under the influence and Steve showed up, out of nowhere, in his old blue Ford Bronco, blaring music with a bunch of guys standing up in the back, holding onto the roll bar, screaming, while sparks flew everywhere from a missing tire. Needless to say, the cop set his sights on a new target, and Jeff and I were released. Steve and his passengers were all high on a variety of hallucinogens and other drugs and thought the sparks from the rim were hilarious. He was hog-tied and escorted away with the cops. I ignored his reckless nature, zero fear of authority, and need to be wild and free, and yearned to be with him. I married him despite these character flaws and worked to create the life I thought I wanted—one filled with luxuries, ease, and comfort.

However, no matter how much older he got, no matter how expensive his suits were, and no matter how polished our life appeared to those on the outside, Steve was always still the guy in the three-wheeled Bronco. He was forever chasing the high, living dangerously, with a total lack of regard for authority. Meanwhile, I had become the mother to a baby girl and had a second child on the way, an experience that offered me a very sobering look at our lifestyle, with its wild parties and lavish spending. Not being able to drink while pregnant and, after our son was born, while nursing, gave me some much-needed perspective about where our life was and where it was going. The verdict: It was totally out of control and heading toward a fall.

One wake-up call came about three weeks after my son was born. My daughter was seventeen months old at the time. I had decided to throw a dinner party, and after the meal was done the kids and I went to bed early. Steve and his friends, however, stayed up all night drinking and doing drugs. At about 6:00 in the morning, the kids and I woke up and went outside to find the men by the outdoor fireplace, surrounded by empty bottles and cigars. When my daughter saw her father, she ran over to him, and he promptly picked her up and brought her into the pool with him—mind you, he was still in the same clothes from the previous night. As he whirled her around in his hazy state,

I held my breath. He thought he was just playing around in a harmless way and joked with his buddies about his toddler being in the pool. But I was not laughing. I was terrified. And at that moment, I knew our lifestyle had to change.

Unfortunately, Steve did not share my desire to recalibrate our home life. He began spending more and more time with a dysfunctional alcoholic couple who lived down the street from us, and consequently we began to drift apart. Around that time, Steve's mood started to shift. He had struggled with bouts of depression before, but this time the disease manifested differently. He became very distant, aggressive, and—one thing I never expected—controlling. He was at the country club 24/7: poker, men's-only golf, happy hour—and don't even get me started about fantasy football. My children and I were always alone. You see, we had built the gilded cage, and unknowingly, I had become the bird—and much of this was my own damn fault.

My Norma Desmond Moment

It is hard for me to fathom that I let myself become so shallow—that I had somehow become obsessed with material things. But no matter how much I acquired, I still felt incredibly empty inside. Life was literally calling out to me from the pit of my stomach, and there was no way I could ignore it. The only thing that would actually fulfill me was the very opposite of what I was doing. I needed to let go, and the only way I could truly live was not to get, but rather to give. I had it all backward, and pretty soon I would learn that I had to give to truly live.

> The only way I could truly live was not to get, but rather to give.

It was yet another night spent lying in bed, staring at the ceiling, crying, and suffering in silence, something I seemed to be doing quite a bit of lately. I looked over at my husband rolled up in a ball, sleeping as far away from me as he could, and wondered how we had come to this. How had two people who loved each other so much, who had been best friends and allies for so long, come to this? On the outside we had it all—the house, the cars, the kids, the money, the fairy-tale love story—but inside we were miles apart, and the distance had become a torturous isolation.

I decided to get up. Wandering into the kitchen, I poured myself a triple Baileys over ice. I never really drank Baileys, but it had been brought over as a gift by a guest at one of our many over-the-top parties and seemed like it would do the trick.

After drinking about half a glass I wandered through the house, ice cubes clinking, and ended up in my walk-in closet. I was naked and decided to put on every piece of jewelry that my husband had ever bought me. I had on my diamond tennis brace-let and matching diamond necklace, my rings, my multiple diamond watches, and just about anything sparkly I could find. I had enough bling on to take out Mr. T. I then slipped into my full-length mink and applied a generous coating of makeup. Glass in hand, I wobbled back into the kitchen and once there, refilled it and sifted through our kitchen junk drawer only to find a leftover clove cigarette from another one of our ridiculous parties.

Even though I didn't normally smoke, I sat outside listening to Grace Potter's song "Nothing But the Water," smoking my clove, sipping my drink, and staring down at thousands of dollars in goods. Mascara running down my face, I listened to the words as they came from Grace's voice: "only the water can help you now." She was referring to a life of sin and desperation being saved by the waters of baptism—a second chance at life. It was like she was singing to me.

I call this my Norma Desmond moment, and it wasn't pretty. I had all of these *things* on me, things that were supposed to make me feel better, and all I felt was empty. I thought I had achieved all that any woman could possibly want. I had it "all," whatever that is. The truth is I was desperately lonely and starting to think that my life was beginning to resemble an episode of *Desperate Housewives*, as the Real Housewives of anything had yet to come out. It was no way to live.

I had it "all," whatever that is.

As I sat there feeling sorry for myself, I realized the words of the song had more meaning to me than I thought. There is a line that goes, "If I give a nickel, I might get a dime." For some reason, it was really sitting with me. Then, I had the "aha" moment that revolutionized my entire worldview and that serves as the foundation for everything I discuss in this book: it takes giving to get, and what you get is far greater than what you give. The words spoke to that pit in my stomach, the inner voice I had been ignoring, the one that was getting loud. It was time for me to listen. Now was the time for change.

Freedom at Camp Rainbow

Over the next year I would open a children's clothing store and throw a charity event in honor of a young boy who lost his battle with cancer. His parents were casual friends of ours, and his mom had always wanted to do something in his honor. So I created a family festival, complete with country music star Collin Raye, and we raised a pretty good size sum of money for charity. Although the young boy had not been treated in Phoenix, it was now where the family called home, so the check went to the Center for Cancer and Blood Disorders at Phoenix Children's Hospital. What happened next would lead me to my destiny.

We went down to the hospital with our giant check, and while touring it I came across a pamphlet, on which was a picture of children—some sick, some well, but all laughing under an image of a rainbow. I asked what it was, and a hospital employee said, "That's Camp Rainbow." She was the director of the camp, and as it turns out, it was a camp run by the hospital for children who have or have had cancer. All I could think of was how badly I wanted to volunteer at that camp. Although the director seemed skeptical about my commitment, she indulged me anyway and took my application, which ended up being accepted. That August of 2003, I packed and prepared to leave my family for eight days and nights and head to the woods of Prescott, Arizona, into the heart of Camp Friendly Pines. I had never been away from my children for more than two nights, and I had never been apart from my husband for more than three. I won't lie—just the thought of it was scary, but something told me I had to do it. That little voice was starting to get louder.

The night before I left for camp was to be a very special one for me. I had asked Steve if we could take the kids, now two years and ten months old, to our country club for a special family dinner. He had promised that we could, and I eagerly rushed through my day picking up last-minute supplies for camp and looking forward to our family outing. When I walked through the door close to the time we needed to leave, there was Steve on the couch with one of his many "illnesses"—manifestations of his clinical depression. I couldn't believe it—not now, not tonight of all nights. Part of me thought, "Oh well, just get a pizza and call it a day." Then that little voice said, "No, no pizza. Take the children out yourself." I had never done that before. Sure, we had eaten lunch or breakfast as a trio, but we had never ventured out to dinner without Steve. So I packed up the kids, put them in the car, and headed up to the country club.

> ## What you are doing now you are soon becoming.

As I pulled up and hopped out of the car, I had the strangest feeling come over me. It was downright eerie. I put my son on my hip and held on to my daughter's hand, and the three of us strolled through the courtyard to our club. As we walked under the archway, I remember feeling like I was in a dream, like we had literally just passed through some ethereal doorway into another world. We sat down, and I put my son in his highchair, handed my daughter her crayons, and it suddenly came over me. I looked at the three of us, and I saw it—I saw three. Just three. Somehow deep down inside me I knew that I was looking at my life as I would soon know it.

There is a sign up at Camp Friendly Pines, where Camp Rainbow is hosted, that hangs in the dining hall, and it reads, "What you are doing now you are soon becoming." In a day I would be sitting under than sign, and I would have no idea how true those words would be.

A Career Is Born

The next couple of years went by pretty quickly, but there was a watershed event that changed the course that my life would follow. At the time, I owned a children's clothing store, was a part-time traffic personality on an ABC-syndicated morning news show, and was also a full-time professional model. My college roommate, who also had moved from California to Arizona, was hosting a charity event called Pardi-Gras under the Palms. There were to be over 300 people in attendance, and she asked me if I could wear a pretty outfit and come pick the winning raffle ticket onstage at the event. I headed to the event completely unaware of what was about to happen.

When I arrived, my friend was in a panic. She had four items to sell onstage, and due to some unexpected circumstance the auctioneer never showed up. She knew I had been a theater major in college and had been to many of my shows, so she told me to get up there and play an auctioneer. I thought she was crazy, but I figured, *Why not?* My stepfather had taken me to a few auctions as a kid, and I used to show up early as a model in the lifestyles tent at the Barrett-Jackson classic car auction just to watch the auctioneers, so I had an idea of what to do. I had also attended several charity events as a guest and even watched the famed auctioneer Jeff Stokes work his magic at Muhammad Ali's Celebrity Fight Night.

With this experience as a spectator and an acting degree under my belt, I headed up onstage and played the auctioneer, and it was brilliant. I felt completely alive and soaked up every minute of the experience. Here I was in a beaded Mandalay bodice top and fitted velvet pants, standing six feet high in my heels, parading around a stage calling bids like some cowboy selling cattle. People ate it up, and bids were flying everywhere. When I walked offstage, I was elated that my little performance was well received, but I was completely caught off guard when people began asking me for my card.

I went about my life and started volunteering at charity auctions with a friend of mine. He was a successful real estate broker who happened to do auctions for kicks on the side. He had gone to auction school and gave me my first real auctioneering lessons. The more I learned and the more gigs I took, the more my little pastime became an obsession.

During this time, my marriage had gone from bad to worse. Facing financial difficulties, we had sold our $2.2 million house and traded it in for a $1.6 million house—ridiculous, I know. My store had been losing money, so I had closed that as well and was looking for concrete ways to really make a living. As it turned out, Jeff Stokes was coming into town to do Muhammad Ali's event again. I pulled a few strings and was able to set up a meeting with Jeff, who got a real kick out of my story about how I became an auctioneer. He told me that if I was absolutely serious about becoming a professional auctioneer, I needed to go to auction school, and he recommended the Western College of Auctioneering in Billings, Montana. He was an instructor there, and classes started in just a few months.

As soon as our meeting was over, I called the school, registered, and prepared myself to head to Billings for fifteen days and stay at the lovely War Bonnet Inn. What transpired over the next several weeks revealed the truth of that sign at the camp cafeteria: "What you are doing now you are soon becoming." Each sixteen-hour day at auction school was fast-paced and pushed me mentally and physically to the point of exhaustion. Just like I did at Camp Rainbow, I shed layers of myself at auction school that helped me find my absolute self. The challenges only cemented my conviction that my future lay in auctioneering.

Starting Over

Coming home from auction school was like coming home from my first Camp Rainbow experience, although this time it was much harder to re-enter my old life. I had caught a glimpse of a different path, and this new perspective cast a much more critical light on the state of my marriage. There were many signs that read "It's time to get out." At that point, my marriage had a worse chance of floating than the Titanic, yet I was still gripping the rail, sinking into the dark, cold sea. Self-delusion is a drug. We can take it over and over just to get by and convince ourselves that everything is fine, when it is really a swirling vortex of crap. I had beautiful kids. I had a beautiful home. I had a closet full of beautiful clothes. And I had a long list of beautiful bullshit excuses of why I was staying.

A few nights after my return, I desperately wanted to talk to Steve. Over the years we had bounced in and out of therapy but were told that it would be difficult to work on our relationship until Steve first addressed his clinical depression. Unfortunately, he couldn't seem to do it. That night, he wouldn't talk to me and instead rolled over and went to sleep with a heavy sigh, as I was used to him doing. I lay there, staring at the ceiling as I had done countless nights before. I felt completely alone and began to cry.

The unspoken truth about misery is that eventually it will end. Only we can decide how and at what moment.

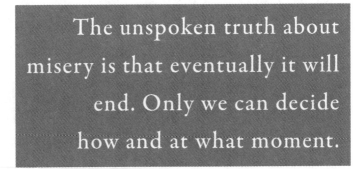

The unspoken truth about misery is that eventually it will end. Only we can decide how and at what moment.

My moment was after dinner one evening. Steve and I were alone. He knew I wanted to talk to him about something important, except his version was me asking him to go on a trip to Hawaii.

"I want a divorce," was not what he expected, or frankly wanted. He was going on a business trip the next morning, so I had timed my request hoping to reduce the opportunity for a big blow-up. I wanted the break to be clean and quiet.

I was lucky that his immediate reaction was shock and contemplation, with just the right amount of denial. In the morning, he woke up, kissed me on my forehead, and said, "We will talk about this more when I return."

On my end, there was nothing to discuss. For the sake of my sanity and the integrity of my soul, I needed to break out of the prison that my life had become. I fantasized about what it would be like to be free. In complete contrast to the person I had married, Steve had developed some very strict rules when it came to the house. There was to be no loud music during the day. There were to be no dogs in the bed once he was out of it. My son was not allowed to ride his push car across the travertine floors. And to save on the electric bill, the doors always needed to be shut when the air conditioning was on.

When he left, it was time to free the household from these regulations. I flung the doors and windows wide open and rocked out to my favorite tunes. With the glee and excitement of any Indy racer, my son sped around in his car as fast as his chubby little legs could move. I laid in bed with my dogs and read the paper. This was it, my moment to take control of my life and end my misery. I was free, and this was going to be what my life was going to be like from now on. My life, my rules. His house, his paper, his money.

In 2008, I walked out the door of that multimillion-dollar life with two kids, a mattress, and $12 to my name to start a new chapter for our family. To retain my independence, I took no court-appointed alimony or child support. I knew that if I were going to be truly free from that gilded cage, I needed to create my new reality on my own. I began to live life "absolute," as we say in the auction industry—no reserve, no safety net, no limitations; endless opportunity.

Are You Living an Absolute Life?

- When do you feel most like "yourself"? Describe what you imagine to be your authentic self: What are your core qualities? What are your values? What do you enjoy doing?

- How does the above vision of yourself align with your current reality? Do you feel like the you who you are now differs from your authentic self in any way? Explain.

- If there is a difference between your two selves, how do you account for it? What limitations are keeping you stuck in a life that isn't truly your own?

- What are your greatest fears in life? How have these fears held you back from living the life that you desire? Journal about all the opportunities you've missed because you let fear stand in the way of action.

- Imagine what your life would look like if you took off the reserve you've placed on it. What possibilities would be opened up to you? How could you (and others) benefit?

CHAPTER 2

GIVE WHEN YOU HAVE NOTHING

Give what you have. To someone, it may be better than you dare to think.

—Henry Wadsworth Longfellow

O ur philanthropy is not a real test of our character. A better measuring stick is when we have seemingly nothing and yet offer the world all we have left. This is when true miracles occur.

I am not suggesting that you must be poor to offer value, as I am not referring only to giving financially to others. Nor am I suggesting that those with large fortunes should be giving away everything they have earned. We have so much more to offer the world than our maxed-out credit cards or the change rattling around in the bottom of our purse.

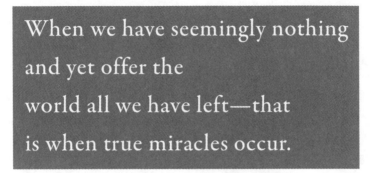

When we have seemingly nothing
and yet offer the
world all we have left—that
is when true miracles occur.

Still, I realize that we tend to associate giving back with people who are already "successful" in the traditional sense of wealth, status, education, etc. Many people wonder, "How can I possibly give something when I have nothing?" That's why I'm not primarily talking about giving money; I'm talking about giving yourself. Even when you think you have nothing left to give—perhaps especially at these times—you can offer the most precious gifts.

Without a Safety Net

When I left Steve, I quickly realized that with my freedom, I was leaving all my material possessions behind. What could I do?

Going back to Steve and the gilded cage was not an option, but no one had told me that outside that cage was a cold, merciless, dead-end alley. I had to borrow from my mother in order to be able to afford my own place. Steve and I had put a $900,000 cash down payment on our $1.6 million house, so I figured I'd have no problem paying her back once our house had sold. However, unbeknownst to me, Steve had taken out a second loan against the house when we had first moved in. This was in 2007, right before the economy crashed. We ended up falling behind on our mortgage payments, and I had even less of a safety net than I realized when I was starting out on my own.

Nonetheless, I got out there and somehow managed to juggle five jobs. I went to a couple I knew who owned a string of night-clubs, and they gave me a gig bartending on Thursday nights. I landed a weekend job in Phoenix doing auctions, and I asked the gal who now owned the retail space that was once mine if I could have a job selling clothes. I still had my modeling agent and picked up work whenever I could, and I would sub in on the local ABC syndicate station for the morning traffic girl whenever she needed a day off or got sick. Basically, I would get off from bartending at 4:00 A.M. on Friday morning, nap a few hours, take the kids to school, report to my retail job, work a full day, come home and crash, then get up at 5:00 A.M. on Saturday to high-tail it to downtown Phoenix to sell salvage vehicles to mechanics in 105-degree heat for $100 a day and fill in for any auctioneer in the warehouse who needed a break. I would work at least five days a week at the shop, take as many modeling jobs as I could get, and be ready to report to the news station by 4:00 A.M. any day on a moment's notice. It was hell, but I wanted to get my new start by myself and on my own terms, without being indebted to Steve for his help.

During this transitional period, I fought hard to keep things normal for my children. I sold all my jewelry in order to buy them furniture and keep food on the table. One day in particular sticks out in my mind as emblematic of our circumstances back then. My children were six and four years old at the time, and they had asked if we could go for ice cream after school. I explained to them that we couldn't do ice cream that day, but for some reason my little boy just couldn't let it go. He kept saying, "Why, Mommy? Why?" I started to cry, and my daughter asked him to "ease up on Mommy."

The truth was, I didn't have the cash it took to buy the ice cream. I barely had enough gas to get to work and no money whatsoever for at least three more days until I got paid. I had canned soup at home to tide us over. So, ice cream was way out of the question.

I wiped away my tears and looked into the rearview mirror at those two little faces and said, "Don't you worry. Tomorrow Mommy will get you ice cream." I had no idea how I was going to do it, but I was not going to break my word to them no matter what. I went home and rummaged through some old things and found some bonds a family member had given the children as a present. I swallowed my pride and walked into the bank with their birth certificates and cashed them out. The bank teller looked at me with disgust as she told me that the bonds had not matured and would be worth only the original value of $25. I told her that my son needed ice cream and she should mind her own business. I picked up the kids from school that day and we went out for our frozen treat. Then, we bought groceries and had a wonderful family meal. It was a great day.

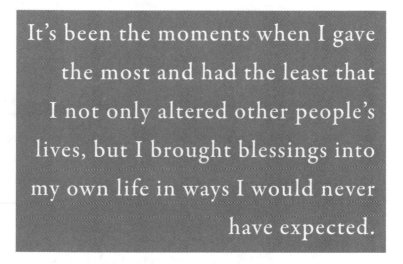

It's been the moments when I gave the most and had the least that I not only altered other people's lives, but I brought blessings into my own life in ways I would never have expected.

Focusing on what I could give my children helped me make it through one difficult day after another as I fought to get back on my feet. More often than not, what I had to offer was not material but rather intangible—an act of service rather than financial generosity. As my kids would say back then, "Daddy has the money, and Mommy has the love." Sometimes it felt like I had such a small well to draw from, but whenever I would find ways to reach out and give to others I would instantly be filled back up. I still volunteered as a counselor at Camp Rainbow every year, even when I was at my lowest point and questioned what I had to offer (as you'll discover later in the book, this wasn't my darkest time yet). But as has been true throughout my life, it's been the moments when I gave the most and had the least that I not only altered other people's lives, but I brought blessings into my own life in ways I would never have expected.

And Mara

Right after I asked for a divorce and was faced with the stark reality of having to build a new life with only $12 to my name, I found myself flipping through my husband's loaned copy of the *Arizona Republic*, contemplating what to do next. Somehow I landed on the obituary page, and a picture of an angelic face stopped my heart for a few beats. The text beside the photo read:

Mara Elise Lois Miskovsky, our Pretty Bird, flew home into the loving arms of Jesus Christ on July 12, 2007. Although she was only with us for 20 months, she forever impacted the lives of all who knew her. We were blessed to share in her contagious laugh and honored to receive her "surprise" kisses. In addition to playing with her big brother and her cousins, Mara loved to read books, snuggle with babies, snap her fingers and dance, swim, and tumble at her gymnastics class. Each morning Mara would climb on top on daddy and mommy to point out the pictures in the paper and remind us that our coffee cups were "hot."

Mara had a great love of food and was always ready to spit out anything she had in her mouth if she came across something she thought would taste better—especially watermelon! Many nights she would chase her daddy across the house to steal his popsicle and then run and hide in the arms of her mommy. We will forever miss her meeting us at the door with a big smile and a sweet kiss. We will cherish the memory of her "happy feet" dance and the way she would point to and name the facial features of anyone who was holding her.

The obituary went on to name those she would meet at heaven's gate and those she was leaving behind. I was undone. Every time I have read it aloud, I find myself sharing tissues with anyone listening. If you have a beating heart in your chest, how could you not be affected? But being moved is not the same thing as taking action.

> Being moved is not the same thing as taking action.

Mara's mother was experiencing tragedy on a scale I could not fathom. Here I was, worrying about where to store all my clothes, and this mother was having to choose the dress to bury her daughter in. I had an issue that I could easily overcome, whereas this mother was dealing with a problem to which there was no solution. I needed to help her, but what could I possibly give?

I began rummaging through my junk drawers. No judgment—you have them too. I was able to scrounge up about $2. I grabbed my kids, went to the nearest drug store, and bought a nice card, and in it I placed a check for $10 from my account that had only $12 in it. I wrote that I felt bad that I could not send more, but I promised that once I got on my feet, I would send more. During a time when she had the right to be selfish and think only of herself, Mara's mother thought of her daughter's piggy noises and fishy faces and asked people to donate to Heifer International and help impoverished families around the world. I was impoverished myself, and I knew I had a chance to change that, but first I needed to help someone in greater need than me. If Mara's mother, Krissy, could give when she was at her lowest and had seemingly nothing left to give, then so could I.

A year and a half later, I was divorced and back on my feet but still not where I needed to be. But it was time to make good on my promise. I found the address from the original obituary and mailed a check for $280. I reminded Krissy that I had promised to send more when I could, but I still apologized that I could not do better just yet. I told her that her little angel was the light I needed that day to push forward and not fall into despair, and I thanked her and Mara for that. Soon after, I received a note in the mail, thanking me for my original letter:

Miss Frye,

I don't know how to begin...I had thank-you notes for over a year now and I still have yet to really start sending them. I feel just awful that I haven't even acknowledged the appreciation we felt for your first gift, and along comes another. I can tell you that I have thought of you many times over the last 16 ½ months. My husband and I shared the card and note you sent with quite a few people, as we truly felt it was kind and generous beyond belief. I have spoken about it in my counseling sessions as proof to me that God is doing all he can to keep us alive. As we travel this path He is paving the way with kindness, generosity, and support from all different sources. You truly personify his grace. Mara was a gift to us. No one child has ever been more loved and wanted than she. As we try to find our way, we never lose sight of the fact that a lifetime of pain is worth the 20 beautiful months we had with her.

We look forward impatiently to a reunion with our baby in God's Kingdom. We know in our hearts that she in a place that is overflowing with love and goodness. I would be lying if I said that it makes it all okay. Be we are grateful to God that He keeps her until we arrive. I will look for you and your family there as well. Surely, you are moved by Him—there isn't any other way to explain such selflessness. We have forwarded your gift to Mara's endowment at Heifer.

You will change the lives of so many people, both in your community and throughout the world. Here with your kindness and support, and there with the confidence and security of being self-reliant. Again, words cannot express how much you touched our family. Please know that the beautiful little girl you have honored was an amazing personality, a kind soul, and the cutest little lovebug you could ever imagine! Your gift of self could not have been used for a better person. She is amazing and you are too. I could go on forever about how special Mara Elise Lois is and how you are made from a mold that not people are—so few in fact. You will always be remembered by our family. Please accept this thank you that seems so inadequate. You have brought a moment of joy to a family that lives in great sadness and indescribable anguish each and every day.

With great admiration, respect, and love,

In His Name,
Krissy, Greg and Grantham

We were moving in synchronicity, resonating with each other at some deep cosmic level, without ever having met. A few days later, I saw a black SUV in line at the same school as my son. I could not see who was driving, but I did notice the license plate read, "ANDMARA." The coincidence would have been too great for this to be Mara's mother, but as I drove away, I remembered something important about myself: I did not believe in coincidences.

The next day I parked and waited for the SUV, anxious to see its owner. Finally, I found the vehicle and parked next to it. A lady emerged from the school and began to head toward the SUV. As she came closer, I could see that her resemblance to Mara was undeniable.

I got out of my car, greeted the woman, and asked, "Are you Krissy? Are you Mara's mom?"

She seemed a little afraid and responded, "Yes, why?"

"I am Letitia Frye," is all I responded because nothing else could come out. My throat was frozen with tears and emotion. Krissy was apparently in the same condition because she could not get out a complete sentence either. We embraced amid silent tears.

"How did you know?" she finally asked.

"It was your license plate," I admitted.

She nodded and said, "Yes, that is for our pretty bird. She loved going on trips to places like Disneyland, so we had the license plate made to take her along with us no matter where we went. 'And Mara.'"

We cried some more, hugged again, and eventually said our goodbyes. I have not seen or heard from her since, but I know we are each imprinted on one another's hearts.

Little did I know I was walking in the footsteps of my soon-to-be hero Danny Thomas. He never welched on his promise, and it changed the world. When he was at his lowest, he gave all he had to those who had even less than him. His legacy was to become the pathway to my future.

A Pledge to St. Jude[1]

Amos Jacobs was one of nine kids in an immigrant family. He changed his name to Danny Thomas, a combination of two of his brothers' names, when he began his career in show business.

When his brother Danny (from whom he borrowed his name) was only a few days old, a rat got into his crib and bit him. Baby Danny screamed and then went into convulsions and was rushed to the hospital. The doctors had a grim prognosis: Baby Danny was going to die. Danny's family was Catholic, and so his mother did the one thing she could—she prayed.

She dropped to her knees and promised God that if he spared her baby, she would beg alms for a year. Making deals with God should never be taken lightly. God has a very long memory and does not forget—unlike your Uncle Marty, from whom you borrowed ten bucks last year with the promise to pay him right back.

Danny's mother prayed through the night, and because of her faith she did not feel hopeless or fearful. She knew that God would hear and answer her prayer. From her perspective, to doubt God was a sin, and to give in to hopelessness was to give in to the devil. Baby Danny recovered, and his mother was true to her word. Every day for a year she went door to door and begged for pennies for the poor. She stood by her promise—a commitment that resonated with Danny Thomas later in life.

Danny Thomas's dream was to be an entertainer. He worked hard those first years and married a woman named Rose Marie. Then, in June 1940, his life changed. At the time, he was making two dollars a night as an MC at a Detroit supper club, the Club Morocco. One night, he received terrible news, especially for a young man with a baby on the way: the club was closing. He had no other job prospects. His wife told him he needed to quit the entertainment industry and get a steady job in the grocery business. Danny's heart was broken, and he began to give in to despair.

The last night the club was open, a man walked in and began giving out cards and telling people the story of his wife. She had been diagnosed with cancer and was facing a surgery and possible death. Like Danny's mother, this man would not accept death as the only answer, so he knelt on the cold stone floor in the hospital and began to pray the same prayer over and over again to Saint Jude, known alternately as "the patron saint of the hopeless" or "the patron saint of the impossible."

The next morning, the doctors were perplexed and dumbfounded. The man's wife was healed and cancer-free. They could not provide him with any medical explanation, but the man knew it was his faith that had healed her. Danny Thomas took one of the man's cards, and on it was a prayer to St. Jude. Danny returned home that night depleted and afraid of what his future held. Was it a sign from God that he was not meant to be an entertainer? Maybe he should listen to his wife and talk to the grocer in the morning. Danny was conflicted because his real passion was entertainment, but his commitment was to support his family.

Danny went to a church to pray for help and direction. He was going to leave an offering and reached into his pocket and found the card with the prayer to Saint Jude. He took the card and beseeched the intervention of St. Jude with a vow. He did not ask for money or fame, only direction in his life. He made the promise to St. Jude that he would build a shrine in his honor.

The next day, Danny Thomas took his wife to his parents' home and decided that he was going to try his luck with the entertainment industry one last time. He was headed to Cleveland, where he knew some people who might be able to help him get back into show business. Something pulled at his mind and weighed on his heart, and at the crossroads he turned left instead of right—toward Chicago rather than Cleveland.

He started off in radio, then became a character actor, and eventually went into stand-up comedy at a converted car showroom called the 5100 Club. He paid his dues, and soon people were lining up to see him. Success was finally within his reach.

Over the next few years, his popularity and career grew, and with that he forgot his vow to St. Jude. However, St. Jude had not forgotten Danny. Leaving a church service one Sunday morning, Danny found in a pew a nine-day novena to, you guessed it—Saint Jude. Chicago was St. Jude's town; it even has the first national shrine to him—in Our Lady of Guadalupe Church in South Chicago. Holding this novena card, Danny contemplated what kind of shrine he would build, but over time the plans were set aside to continue building his career on the stage and silver screen.

Then one night, Danny had a dream in which he saw a little boy injured in a terrible car accident and rushed to a hospital. The doctors would not treat the boy, and he ended up dying on the stretcher. It felt so real for Danny that it haunted him for days, and from this came an idea.

He remembered the man whose wife had cancer. He prayed on the cold floor of his room for help. He recalled his own mother praying for his brother and vowing to ask for alms if God would help her. Through these experiences, Danny Thomas began to have a vision of a St. Jude's shrine as a place for the ill and infirm who had lost all hope, but he had no idea what his dream would become.

Eventually, he decided that in his shrine, St. Jude would watch over the children with incurable diseases so that as many as possible could overcome the odds and live, while also providing hope and sanctuary for their families. This vision led to the founding of St. Jude Children's Research Hospital in Memphis, Tennessee. There was one more important aspect to this place of miracles: not only would it be open to every child, but no family would ever be asked to pay for anything.

Danny Thomas went on to use his platform and name to raise the money to build the hospital and properly fund it. He had become his mother, going door to door, begging for pennies as part of a vow to help heal a child.

Has Danny Thomas's word outlived him? You bet it has, and it will continue to do so lifetime after lifetime after lifetime. That is the power of working to create a legacy before you can fund it. As any auctioneer for nonprofits will tell you, there are plenty of people who are happy to share their money to better the world around them. All you need is devotion to the task at hand. Like Danny Thomas and his mother before him, you must make a promise and then follow it through to completion regardless of the obstacles that threaten to throw you off-course.

Realize, too, that no act of compassion is too small to matter. You don't have to found a charitable organization to make a difference. Sometimes even the tiniest offerings bring the biggest and most meaningful rewards.

Your Word = Your Value

The ancient Egyptians believed that you could take your material possessions with you when you died, so they built monuments, filled them with riches, invited their "forever" friends to join them, and then sealed the chamber, hoping someday to be put on display in a museum. They tried to bring everything they valued in this world with them into the next one.

I don't believe that we can take any material objects with us when we die. I am more of an "ashes to ashes" sort of gal. My focus is on what I leave behind, the impression I leave on the world. It is about how I can help others—as many as I can. That is the greatest legacy I can create.

What is it that we bring to the world that has value? Shiny things? Money? Status? It is interesting that we want these things, but they're not what we value. Have you ever asked a dollar bill for a favor? If you were in a tight corner and needed a friend, would you call up your car and ask it for help?

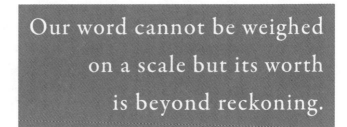

Our word cannot be weighed on a scale but its worth is beyond reckoning.

What does have true value—more than gold, more than the perfect area code to live in, more than the latest iPhone model in your hand—is someone having your back. Our word cannot be weighed on a scale but its worth is beyond reckoning. It is an appreciating asset. The more we use it, the greater its value.

In Danny Thomas's story and in my own, we made a pledge. In Danny's case it was with a saint, and in mine it was with a grieving mother. No one was holding us accountable in either situation, so it could have been a "piecrust promise," to use Mary Poppins's term. Yet both of us kept our promise, and two very important things happened as a result: our value as human beings increased, and something new and miraculous grew out of our commitment. Danny created a new sanctuary for families and children that would continue to spread across the country and provide hope without the financial stress that comes with pediatric illnesses. My gift for Mara helped heal broken hearts, including my own.

> "That's a piecrust promise—
> easily made, easily broken."
> —Mary Poppins

Sometimes all we have to give others is our word, but that in and of itself is an incredibly important offering. Your word should never be given lightly. It defines what we are capable of and determines how we establish our value. I have seen women getting out of bad relationships struggle to obtain a job, and they want to give up because they don't think they have anything to offer. They lack a job history, a high school education, and worst of all, they lack hope. But every single one of us has our word, and that is a priceless offering. We can commit to giving of ourselves, even when we feel empty, lost, and lacking.

No matter where you are in life, you can build equity through your deeds. I share this with people I meet who tell me that they don't have enough of something they think they need in order to take action. Their sense of limitations becomes the barrier preventing them from breaking through to their fullest potential. They are held back by mere excuses, all beginning with the phrase "I don't have enough..." "I don't have enough money, time, experience, beauty, intelligence, etc." These are the self-constructed boxes in which we place ourselves. At minimum, self-limiting beliefs can keep us from getting a better job and making more money. In the worst-case scenario, they can prevent someone from leaving an abusive situation—in other words, putting a reserve on their life.

This is when your word can open up your world. You can help others, volunteer, and provide value to other people's lives. You will not be forgotten. People will promote you, give you referrals, and have your back when you need it. They will speak of your character and your trustworthiness. Many times, this is enough for someone else to give you a chance in a new job or position. But regardless of the external responses to your commitment, the gift of your word liberates you by opening your heart to gratitude and generosity and removes the reserve on your life. Looking outward to serve others will draw you out of your darkest times and fill you up when you feel completely empty. Keeping your word is free, but it pays dividends.

> Your word can
> open up your world.

Ask yourself: What can you commit to giving today—right now, this very moment? We all have talent. We all have time. We all have attention. We all have compassionate acts. All of these things—and more—we can offer the world, even when it seems to us that we have nothing. We must dig deep and cultivate an awareness of what is going on around us. Learn to ask others what they need and offer to help in places that angels fear to tread. When you are in the service of others, giving of your time and talents, asking nothing in return, you will gain true perspective on your life.

> Keeping your word is free,
> but it pays dividends.

Are You Giving Fearlessly and Honoring Your Word?

- What do you have to offer the world right now, as you are? Think beyond money and material items— how can you give of yourself? Who would benefit from those blessings? For every item, tangible or intangible, that you can give, make a plan to share your gift with a specific person, group, or organization.

- How do you honor your word? Analyze the promises you give to people, no matter how small they are. Do you tell people what they want to hear or do you tell them the truth? For example, if someone asks you if you are available to go out to dinner on Friday and you either don't want to go or have another commitment—do you tell them sure, you will go, thinking you will have plenty of time to think of an excuse to get out of it, or do you tell them the truth up front? Sometimes giving your word or withholding a promise can be uncomfortable, but if it was always easy, then it would not be much of a character builder.

- To what lengths have you gone to keep your word? Giving your word becomes a contract between you and the person to whom you gave it. How have you fulfilled that contract? It is not always easy or fun. Therefore, you should not give your word lightly unless you are sure you can keep it or, more importantly, intend to keep it. Sometimes we must go way outside our comfort zones to do what we promise. If you say to your child that you are going to sell 100 boxes of Girl Scout cookies, then you better have a good plan. You may find yourself in an undersized brown uniform hawking your cookies door to door. Yes, I am talking to you dads out there too.

- Look for opportunities to give your word and help someone else when they need it. Maybe it is babysitting their cat while they leave to see their sick mother for a few days. Maybe it is helping someone but cutting their grass because they have physical limitations. Maybe it is putting in a good word for someone to help them get a job. You make the promise to help, and then you do it. It is not any more complicated than that.

Note

1. Many different versions of the Danny Thomas story exist. I choose to use Danny's own words about the inspiration behind St. Jude Children's Research Hospital: https: //www.guideposts.org/faith-and-prayer/prayer-stories /power-of-prayer/guideposts-classics-danny-thomas-on -keeping-his.

CHAPTER 3

VISUALIZE THE EXACT LIFE YOU WANT

The clearer you are when visualizing your dreams, the brighter the spotlight will be to lead you on the right path.

—Gail Lynn Goodwin

Life is too short to spend it making small talk, even with strangers. Oftentimes when I first meet people, especially at the beginning of a mentoring relationship, I'll ask them a simple, and yet somehow unsettling, question: "So, what do you want?"

Cue the crickets.

This question tends to generate a blank stare. To break the silence, I provide some additional prompting: "If I were a genie in a bottle and could grant you whatever you want, what would your life look like? I mean, what do you *really* want?"

It's amazing how many people either don't know what they want or aren't able to get into specifics. I usually hear the same generic answers: "more money," "more freedom," etc. When pressed to give me more details, most people are unable to do so—at least, it will take them a while to get there.

Aim with Intention

If this happens, I ask the person to use pen and paper—not electronics; they must get out a writing utensil—to write out exactly what they want and exactly what their life looks like. I also instruct them that if they truly have no idea what it looks like, they should write down exactly what they *don't* want their life to look like. By doing this, they will inadvertently draw a clear picture of what they *do* want in life.

Why should it be handwritten? Well, that derives from being a volunteer camp counselor to children with cancer for over ten consecutive years. One of the activities the children are taught is archery, which is a brilliant way to exercise their minds, develop motor skills, and build confidence. On my first night of volunteer orientation at camp, we had to do a scavenger hunt that included shooting an arrow through a balloon in the dark to pop it and obtain our next clue. Now mind you, these volunteer counselors were all former campers, all cancer survivors, and all far younger than me. A lot of them had been disfigured or left with disabilities from their treatment. So you must understand my amusement when my band of merry players, consisting of a one-legged nineteen-year-old girl, a half-blind twenty-year-old boy, a girl using a walker, and a few other young injured cancer warriors, took up those bows and basically convinced me that this camp was secretly training assassins. Every single one of their arrows hit the balloon with just one shot.

You see, that is the secret. An arrow can hit the mark only with *intention*. After many years of camp, I too became an archer, and one of the first things you learn in this sport is to clear your mind and focus solely on your target, then release the arrow with intention, and *bulls-eye!* That is why you use pen and paper when writing down exactly what you want and exactly what your life looks like. Writing your vision by hand forces you to clear your mind and become laser-focused. You are the arrow, and your ideal life and best version of yourself is the mark. You must visualize the target with a specificity that causes all distractions and potential challenges to fade into the background. You have to have intention to hit that mark.

> An arrow can hit the mark only with *intention*.

Allow me to elaborate on why those overly broad answers like "more money" and "more freedom" are unhelpful when it comes to goal-setting. The less specific you are, the less intention you give your life. I once had a woman answer my question like this: "Well, I suppose I would like fewer obligations and more time to myself," to which I replied, "So you are basically telling me that you would like to end up arrested, in jail, in solitary confinement, and you'd be living your ideal life?" Of course that is not what she meant, but leaving your intentions that vague can make that saying "Be careful what you wish for" come true in wildly unexpected ways.

You need to visualize your goals in concrete details. I appreciate the story Earl Nightingale used to tell about what ships can teach us about having direction in life. Having been raised near a harbor, Nightingale spent a lot of time as a child on the docks watching the vessels come and go from the ports. He explains the lesson he derived from this activity:

> Ships operate the way people ought to, I believe, but so few do. Maybe you've never given it much thought, but at any given moment, a ship has a direction. That is, she's sailing to a predetermined port of call, or she's in port, getting ready to sail to another one. You can climb up to the navigation bridge of a big, far-sailing ship and ask the captain where he's going. He can tell you instantly—and in one sentence.[1]

Just like the captain can tell you "instantly—and in one sentence" where he or she is taking that ship, you must be able to state your goals without hesitation and with enough familiarity to capture them vividly and yet concisely. Otherwise, you will lack the intentionality you need to hit your mark.

Make It Present Tense

A goal is just a wish until it is written down. So step one is a journal—not a diary, but a journal. There is a difference. Both are blank books in which you can write, but one is filled with unfiltered actions, reactions, and emotions, while the other is pure, focused intention. I usually tell people to go to a local bookstore that has an entire section labeled "Journal" and walk around for a while until one jumps out at them. It may have an image or a saying that speaks to them and makes them feel a personal connection to it. Regardless of what draws them to it, they should find a journal in which they will be incentivized to write regularly.

> A goal is just a wish until it is written down.

Next, I ask them to write down everything about their ideal life. Who do they know in this dream life? How do they know them? What job do they have? Where do they live? What does their life look, sound, smell, and taste like? *Be as specific as possible.* For instance, saying you want to live in "a bigger house" isn't precise enough. What sort of bigger house—a two-story, a 3,000-square-foot ranch, a Craftsman-style house, a spacious farmhouse? And where is this house located—in a different town, in a rural or urban location, on a park or a lake? Provide as many details about your ideal life and all its elements as you can.

I will give you a few examples from my own life. You see, I keep all my journals in order to revisit them years later and trace my journey. It's amazing the accuracy of what I wrote down as to what my life is actually like today. Back when I was making just over $20,000 a year and struggling to put food on the table for my family, I journaled about my life as I envisioned it. I wrote down the feeling of my sheets on my body, the sound my children's feet made on the hardwood floors, the smell of gardenia and ylang ylang filling the house, what it was like to walk through the aisle of the organic grocery store and not check the price of the cheese. I wrote about traveling on planes all over the country, performing on stages in front of countless audiences, and noted even what my breathing was like just before I took the stage. I wrote about knowing rock stars on a first-name basis that I grew up listening to on the radio and described the things we joke about.

Notice how I never wrote in the future tense? When I journal, I write in the present tense, detailing my life exactly as I see it—not what I wish it to be, but exactly as I see it to be. By the way, I live in a house with hardwood floors, my candles smell of gardenia and ylang ylang, I never check the price of the cheese, and Alice Cooper loves to tease me about #mysteryblonde. If you don't know that inside joke, just google my name and Johnny Depp, and you will get the picture.

I even went a step further than journaling. Halloween has always been my favorite day of the year, so about twelve years ago, I started a Halloween tradition meant to focus and refine my intentions. The first time I did this, I wrote down exactly what my ideal life looked like, one vision at a time, on small pieces of paper, folded each one up, and then dropped them all into a jar. I lit a candle, burned some sage, and made a ceremony out of it. And then I put the jar away for a year.

The next Halloween, I would grab the candle, the sage, and my jar and sit and unfurl the scraps of paper, reading each vision aloud one by one. If the vision had been achieved and was now my reality, I would burn it. If not, I would put it aside until I was done. Once I had read all the papers, I would reexamine each of the visions from the previous year and decide whether or not they were still my life as I saw it. If they were, I would fold them up and put them back in the jar, along with any new realities I had added that year. If they no longer made sense, I would just rip them up. Then I'd seal the jar and repeat the process the following Halloween.

One day I was in a store and noticed a cute hand-painted jar with a cork lid, and on the top of that lid it said, "A goal is just a wish until it is written down." I almost passed out when I saw it, because that is *exactly* what I wrote when I started this tradition years before. I still have that painted jar, and I still use it for that ceremony every Halloween. And about seven years ago, I invited my children into the tradition, and now we all start each

Halloween together outside with a candle, some sage, and a very wise jar. By the way, one of those first visions in both my journal and that jar involves you reading this book right now. Boom, *bulls-eye!*

So yes, I want you to go out and get yourself a journal, but if that is not accessible to you, just grab a pen and paper—heck, even a napkin will work—and start writing down your life as you see it. There have been so many successful people in this world that swear by this practice. This is not something new, nor is it rocket science, but it works.

Your life needs intention to become all that you see it to be. You need intention to become all that you are meant to be.

In one of my journals from about five years ago, I spoke of all the people I knew in the White House, what my feet felt like as I walked up the steps to the entrance of the building, and so on and so on. The funny thing is, there are more than a dozen people whom I've known for years who are currently living and/or working in the White House, including the president. And that is a shocker—even to me!

Your life needs intention to become all that you see it to be. You need intention to become all that you are meant to be. Every strategy that I give you in this book leads back to the same core idea: keep your intention, stay in the sweet spot, and hit your mark. It is all about the soul, and how to tap into it, in order to be your best self and live an absolute life. The first step is to visualize your life, take pen to paper, and write it down!

What Is Your Ideal Life?

- What do you *really* want? If you encountered a genie in a bottle who offered to make your dream life materialize, what would that dream life look like? Try to answer that question in one sentence.

- Write down, in great detail, everything about your ideal life: Who do you know? What do you do for a living? Where do you live? What does your life look, sound, smell, and taste like? If you struggle to answer this question, proceed to the next one.

- What *don't* you want your life to look like? Be as specific as possible.

- If earlier you were unable to state in one sentence what your ideal life entails, reflect on your answers to the two previous questions and create a statement of intention. For example, it might begin as follows: "In my ideal life, I am..."

- List three things you could do *today* to start aiming toward your dream life.

- List three things you could do *this week* to focus your intentions on the mark of your dream life.

- List three things you could do *this month* to pursue the mark of your dream life.

- List three things you could to *this year* to nail your target—or at least make substantial progress toward it.

Note

1. Earl Nightingale, **Your Success Starts Here: Purpose and Personal Initiative** (Shippensburg, PA: Sound Wisdom, 2019), 18.

CHAPTER 4

PASSION BEFORE PAYCHECK

There is a voice inside of you that whispers all day long, "I feel this is right for me, I know that this is wrong." No teacher, preacher, parent, friend or wise man can decide what's right for you. Just listen to the voice that speaks inside.

—Shel Silverstein

How many of us follow the paycheck rather than the heart? I realize that everybody needs to pay their bills. I'm not asking you not to meet your financial obligations. But if you have found something that brings your life passion—something that truly ignites your soul—then you're going to have to get in and around it before you get paid to do it.

> If you've found something that ignites your soul, get in and around it *now*, before you get paid to do it.

When I started out as an auctioneer, nobody knew who I was. I was a rookie who really needed to work on her chant. Before I went to auction school, I did auctions completely free of charge with my real estate broker friend. While I did not earn any income that way, I learned a lot about what being an auctioneer entailed and was able to gain some valuable experience.

In my first paid auction job I earned $100 a day to sell anywhere from 400 to 800 items and chant for up to nine hours with only two ten-minute breaks. To many people, this sounds completely insane and simply not worth it. The hours versus the pay do not equal out. But because I was so passionate about auctioneering and because of how alive, inspired, and purposeful it made me feel, I was willing to earn next to nothing in order to gain experience and surround myself with those who were already doing it far longer, much better, and for much higher pay than me.

Now, mind you, I had two kids to feed. So I held four other jobs in addition to auctioneering in order to make ends meet. When I moved into benefit auctions, I started doing them for $500 while other auctioneers were making $5,000. I understood that I was not as good as those other auctioneers...not yet, that is. What I needed was time and experience—time in and around the very thing and people doing what it was that set my soul on fire. Eventually, as I developed my skills and had more auctions under my belt, I was able to let go of other jobs. But this experience taught me a crucial lesson: if you really want to succeed at something, you can't wait for the payoff to make sense for you to dedicate yourself to that endeavor. You must put in the time and the work to immerse yourself in the thing that you want the most. You can't just walk through the door of a new profession and expect to get a paycheck equal to what the pros have rightfully earned. The secret to eventually making what they make—heck, blowing right past them—is your willingness to put passion before a paycheck.

> If you really want to succeed at something, you can't wait for the payoff to make sense.

Make Your Biggest Break

There are many stories of famous individuals who have fol-lowed this practice to achieve extraordinary success. At the age of fifteen, Barbra Streisand negotiated a deal with Anita and Alan Miller at the Cherry Lane Theater in Greenwich Village to babysit their children in exchange for a scholarship to their act-ing school. There was no paycheck involved, just her passion. In lieu of going to college, she worked office jobs while taking acting lessons and eventually entered a talent night at a local club. Last time I checked, people don't get paid to enter talent contests. But that night led to a career as a cabaret singer, and the rest, as they say, is history.

Or consider David Geffen's story. After quitting college to pursue his passion in the entertainment business, he was turned down for job after job until he finally landed a gig in the mail-room at the William Morris Agency. He used his time in the mailroom to network with as many people as possible, and even-tually he became a talent agent. Fifty years and $6 billion later, he has earned himself a spot in the Rock & Roll Hall of Fame.

It is amazing what will happen when you align your life with your passion. My biggest breaks came from unexpected circum-stances—from situations where I wasn't chasing a paycheck but rather was pursuing my interests and prioritizing giving over getting.

This first one came when I was asked to volunteer during the Super Bowl at an auction to benefit St. Jude Children's Research Hospital in honor of Nicky Maillard, a boy who had passed away from cancer. He had been treated at Phoenix Children's Hospital (PCH) and St. Jude Children's Research Hospital. Nicky's mother Lisa knew me from my involvement in the PCH community, and she called me a week before the event, asking me to volunteer my services at it. Now at the time, I was doing maybe ten to twenty charity events a year, but I was still mainly working in the warehouse selling salvage cars in the heat—in Spanish—for $100 a day. So, it wasn't a point in my life when it was easy for me to do a gig for free: I was out of poverty, but I still was only making the bare minimum to survive on as a family of three in the Phoenix area. I agreed to do the event, not realizing that performing at it would be the fuel that launched my career.

> My biggest breaks came when I was prioritizing giving over getting.

What I didn't know at the time—in fact, what I didn't learn until a year ago—is that there was a very famous auctioneer slated to perform at Lisa's fundraiser. His son was a close friend of Nicky's family, so his father had volunteered for the event. However, one week before the auction, the father was diagnosed with throat cancer and out of necessity had to back out. I didn't recognize the magnitude of the event; at the time, I thought I was simply doing a friend a favor, but my desire to give and my passion for auctioneering drove me to do my very best. So, I researched the statistics and the foundations being supported by the charity event, and I helped Lisa make a lot of money that night in memory of her son.

I had made business cards prior to this and passed them out when requested. Little did I know that one of these cards would find its way into the hands of someone at the St. Jude Fundraising Office in Southern California, which would make for my second big career break. When my cell phone rang, I was sitting in the boutique at my retail job. The woman on the line said she was calling on behalf of the Beverly Hills office of St. Jude Children's Research Hospital. She had heard that I'd been doing a wonderful job at other charity auctions and requested that I work at an upcoming event for them in Los Angeles. St. Jude had always held a special place in my heart. Several children at Camp Rainbow had been treated at St. Jude, and as I kid I used to watch Marlo Thomas, Danny Thomas's eldest daughter, on television. I was passionate about the organization's cause and loved that no child would ever be denied treatment based on their inability to pay.

So here's what I did: I borrowed a dress from the store in which I worked, agreed to do the event for $500, arranged babysitting for my children, and took a chance and went to LA. When I arrived at the event, I noticed a man who looked a bit like Dick Van Dyke singing "Chim Chim Cher-ee" during sound check onstage. Still not quite grasping the magnitude of the event I was about to do, I went ahead and changed into my borrowed dress, swallowed my fear, removed my limitations, and headed backstage. Standing there, it was then that I realized the man right next to me actually *was* Dick Van Dyke. Perhaps no surprise in hindsight, considering I was at one of the largest star-studded Hollywood fundraisers run by Danny Thomas's children: Runway for Life. I was scheduled to follow a four-year-old girl with cancer singing an acapella rendition of "Somewhere over the Rainbow." After she sang, she handed me the mic and wished me "good luck" in a darling little tone.

That night we made history. We sold only three items, but together with the Give to Live program we raised just shy of $1 million. After this performance in Beverly Hills, my career changed on a dime and my brand took off like a rocket ship across America. Today, St. Jude Children's Research Hospital is my largest client.

> Are you limiting the possibility of life as you envision it because you're setting a reserve on your efforts?

On a side note, if you're wondering what a big-name non-profit like St. Jude was doing hiring an auctioneer seven days prior to the actual event, it's because their usual auctioneer—one of the leading auctioneers for Sotheby's nationwide—was struck by a car when she was out riding her bicycle the day before, and her jaw had to be wired shut. If I had not removed my reserve and faced my fears, then I would have missed the greatest chance and opportunity for my success. I am not suggesting that I was capitalizing on tragedy; rather, I had worked hard and was prepared when opportunities opened their doors to me. Without continued hard work, these would have been one-time events. What I capitalized on was using the opportunities to show what I could do and then do it with passion. It's amazing what pathways open for you when you're looking to grow, gain experience, and give back, rather than simply get a paycheck.

Are You Putting Passion Before Paycheck?

- Are you limiting the possibility of life as you envision it because you're setting a reserve on your efforts? What opportunities have you turned down simply because they didn't pay what you thought they ought to?

- How do you determine what's worth your time? How *should* you evaluate this?

- What volunteer opportunities exist in the industry or the cause that ignites your passion? How can you contribute your time and services to gain experience and grow in this area or simply to feel more fulfilled?

- What are some ways that you can hone your skills by donating or providing them at a low cost? How might smaller gigs, networking opportunities, or giveaways help propel you along your career trajectory?

CHAPTER 5

APPRECIATE BOTH LIFE'S LANDMINES AND ITS ROSES

Change is inevitable. Change is constant.

—Benjamin Disraeli

G athered around the dinner table every night, my children and I play a game called "Roses and Thorns." In order to share about our day, we tell each other what the "roses" in it were—the positives, the opportunities, the pockets of joy—as well as what the "thorns" were—the challenges, the prickly points of the day. This activity enables us to celebrate and express gratitude for the good in our lives while also finding support and an action plan for the difficulties. It energizes and focuses us, it brings us closer together as a family, and it is a much-anticipated part of our nightly routine.

Over the years, I've adapted the title of the game as I've shared its spirit with mentees and audiences to say that life isn't made up of roses and thorns; it's a road full of roses and landmines. In other words, don't expect a perfect life, but work to create a full one. Realize that if you're in a difficult period, there will be freedom from it down the road. Similarly, if you're on the upswing, don't get cocky or overly comfortable: pride does in fact come before the fall. I thought I was living the life of my dreams when I was married to Steve, but when I got out of that marriage I was left worrying about how to afford even basic items.

> Don't expect a perfect life,
> but work to create a full one.

This awareness of the balance of life and the need to temper our emotions when in one phase of it does not mean that we should live a careful, restricted life. Absolutely not—you *never* want to set a reserve on yourself. What it does mean is that we must broaden our viewpoint to see life in its messy fullness and to draw on our inner strength to navigate through the landmines to get to the soil where roses grow. Without this perspective, I could not have endured my traumatic brain injury, the loss of the father of my children, or the loss of my plus-one child.

Thanksgiving with a Head Trauma

My career as an auctioneer had taken off following the St. Jude event in LA, and in an ironic turn of events I had reconnected with my college boyfriend Jeff and was in a serious relationship with him. Everything was finally coming together: I had become highly sought-after in my industry, I had a healthy romantic relationship, Steve and I were successfully navigating the murky waters of co-parenting, and I was making enough money to give my family a comfortable living. Then, on November 27, 2014, I encountered yet another landmine—one that would literally knock me off my feet and leave my head spinning for years to come.

It was Thanksgiving morning. The plan was to have breakfast with Steve and our children before he would drop us off at the airport for a 1:00 P.M. flight to have Thanksgiving dinner with Jeff and his family. I began the day by calling my father—a man with whom I had only recently begun talking after repairing our relationship—to sing him happy birthday with my kids. Heading out for a "quick jog," I heard the phone ring again: it was my dad, calling to tell me he had a terrible premonition about me and to be extra careful that day. I brushed it off and headed outside for my run.

Running was—and still is—a way of life for me. At the age of forty-four, I was averaging thirty-five to forty miles per week. My children were eleven and twelve at the time, so I felt comfortable leaving them at home while I jetted out at 10:30 A.M. for a quick three miles—a short run that should have taken only twenty-five or so minutes. Steve would be over at 11:00 A.M., so I thought this would be the perfect distance to put me home ahead of him and allow me time to shower while he hung out with the kids.

As runners, we always know the possibility of being hit by a car. In fact, I don't know of any serious runners who have never entertained the thought. So as I approached the crosswalk at 10:43 A.M. to see a black Audi stopped at the intersection with the driver looking north as two cars were barreling south toward us at fifty-five to sixty miles an hour, I simply did that silly jog-in-place thing that makes people laugh at runners who are waiting at crosswalks. I did what runners (and everyone else crossing a street) are always told to do: I waited. I looked both ways. Then, just as those two cars were right about to pass the Audi, I stepped into the crosswalk, thinking there was no way the driver would make a move. After all, he had been fully stopped there for a while. I figured that he must have seen me. What I didn't know was that the driver was on his way to meet his girlfriend's parents for the first time and help with the Thanksgiving meal preparation. He was supposed to be there at 10:30 A.M. Just as I stepped into the crosswalk, he looked at his watch and saw that it was 10:43 A.M., so he made the decision that I never saw coming...he gunned his engine to beat those two cars heading south.

This part of the story is very difficult to share. The next thing I know, I feel the heat of the car's front grill approaching me. Everything from this moment on seems to move in slow motion—a lot like pieces of film being played back after the fact. The heat became more intense as it reached the point of impact, and I recall thinking, "This is happening. This is real. *Let go*." Something inside told me just to relax, not stiffen up, and simply accept what was happening. As the car hit my left side, I was thrown up into the air. Everything seemed to stand still, frozen in time. Once I hit the car, I was upside down looking at the driver. His eyes were so wide that they were almost cartoon-like. His face was marked by sheer terror. I can only imagine what he saw in mine.

Next, the faint sound of blood-curdling screaming from across the street. Just before impact, I recall seeing a woman and her dog walking down the sidewalk. I think it may have been her; I really don't know. What happened afterward exists in my mind as fragments of recollections, pieced together into a slightly more coherent memory over the years. I remember hitting the windshield. I remember the sound and smell of burning rubber as the driver pulled his car as hard as he could away from those oncoming cars in order to bring my body away from them. Although it has been over four years, those tire marks are still there today, etched onto the road as a reminder of the trauma.

Then, blackness.

When I came back to consciousness, I realized I was on the ground. There was a high-pitched ringing in my ears like you hear in those war movies after a deafening blast. The pain in my head was extreme, unlike anything I can express in words. I looked around and saw the driver emerging from his vehicle—again, seemingly in slow motion. I saw my shoes in two different places on the road, my iPhone smashed to pieces and at a distance from me, my baseball cap several feet in another direction, and my earphones halfway in. I was so disoriented. All I could do is keep repeating, "I am so sorry." The driver had his door ajar and was trying to say something to me, but although his mouth was moving I could not hear anything other than the persistent ringing in my ears. I think he might have been asking me if I was okay, to which I believe I responded, "Yes, I think so, but my head..." I reached my hand back to touch the source of my pain and felt something so uncannily warm and gelatinous. Drawing my hand back, I saw blood—a lot of it—and tissue. I passed out.

Here is where it gets interesting because I can remember everything from this point forward in incredible detail. I felt such peace—a peace beyond anything expressible in language. It was like I was falling through a hole in time, and as I fell, I did not feel afraid. It didn't really even feel like I was falling at all— it was more like a floating sensation, even though I was moving downward rapidly. Suddenly, I landed in the most beautiful field. I could hear the soft, gentle sound of wheat swaying in the breeze. The sun was illuminating the landscape, casting warm, vibrant rays on the ground beneath it. I had never experienced such joy and complete and utter peace. I looked down and saw my favorite childhood sneakers—a pair of red Keds. I saw myself as a four- or five-year-old child. All of a sudden, it dawned on me where I was: it was my Aunt Justine's farm in Pennsylvania, a place my father took me to before a messy divorce ended visitations. That farm had always been my "heaven on earth." I would play and hide in those fields all day. I've never felt freer and more alive in any place than I did on that farm. And this experience there was no different: it was glorious, and I felt like I could stay there forever.

Then, something happened. It was like a unison of voices said, "No, not yet." I fought it; I wanted to stay there so badly, stay in the serenity, but now the voices were pushing me—not physically pushing me, but propelling me upward somehow, back to the place from which I had fallen. It was like a tunnel. I said, "No! Please, no," but a kind, soothing voice responded gently but firmly, "No, you must go." As I emerged from the tunnel, I could see my body on the road beneath me being picked up and carried to the sidewalk by the driver who had hit me. I saw people being pushed aside as a loud noise approached. From in front of me I heard a muffled voice attempting to speak with me—at first it sounded garbled, like one of the adult characters in *Peanuts*. Soon it became apparent that the voice was from a fireman asking, "Are you alright? Can you hear me?"

I had been unconscious, but yet I had never felt more conscious. What happened from here onward was a whirlwind. The emergency medical technicians asked me a series of questions, mostly ones that just seemed to irritate me: "What season is it? Who is the president?" and so on. Then I heard, "Wrap her up! Let's GO!" I had fundraised once to build a level-one trauma unit and remember after volunteering there for a day that level-one trauma patients only have so many minutes to receive help before their damage is permanent. I also know why the room is so expensive to build: you can't move a level-one trauma patient from room to room for any tests. All the equipment must be in one room and on swinging arms to come down to the patient. The bay of the room must be large enough to fit every specialist in one place. Because the patient cannot be moved, everything and everyone must be able to move to the patient. I would soon find out why.

> I had been unconscious, but yet I had never felt more conscious.

Prior to this incident I had always had a photographic memory and could go "off book" for any of my performances. I would use word associations to trigger my memory while onstage. This little game I played in my career was about to save my life. While in the back of the ambulance, I went into shock. I heard an officer attempting to ask me questions, but no matter how hard I tried to answer them I just kept coming up blank. I was a Jane Doe. I had no ID and no idea who or where I was. Then I spotted the officer's name tag: it said Brown—Officer Brown. I knew that was a color. I immediately latched onto that memory, and my brain seemed to follow suit. I said, "Your name is a color." I gasped. "I am a mother. Oh my God! I am a mother. I have two kids." It was like playing Pictionary. Suddenly things started coming back into clarity. Then I blurted out: "My two kids—they're home alone." I remember the officer's eyebrows began to raise, so I continued: "They are old enough, and I live close...Oh my God, they have a father, and he lives close!" All of a sudden, memories came flooding in. I handed the officer my smashed phone and demanded, "Call kids' dad." He did, and then he handed the phone back and we were off like lightning.

The ambulance ride seemed to take forever. They could not get a needle in my arm because my veins were collapsing. I had been on the road working for eight days straight and was exhausted and dehydrated. They were now up to twelve-gauge needles. It was like a horror show with bits of comedy intermixed. Out of nowhere, my phone began playing the Barry White song I had been running to, and it would not turn off. It was like an absurdist play or a bizarre nightmare. The longer we rode, the more I started to panic. I knew we had passed plenty of hospitals, and that's when it dawned on me that we must be heading to a level-one trauma unit. That meant I was screwed.

I don't remember much else from that ambulance ride except one big white EMT who kept telling me not to pass out. I was trying so hard to fight...I could not stop thinking about my kids, but the adrenaline was wearing off and reality and weakness were starting to set in. The EMT looked at me and held my face as we came to a stop, and he instructed, "Letitia, we are about to get out of here, and when we do there's going to be a lot of people waiting for you, and things are going to get real scary, and I just need you to fight. I am going to tell you three things and ask you to repeat them. Then I will find you later today and ask you what they are again. Are you ready, Letitia?"

I nodded yes.

"Brian, green ball, fifteen. Did you hear me? Brian, green ball, fifteen."

I nodded again. Then I did the trick I do onstage to remember my script—word association. When I was fifteen, I dated a boy named Brian, and I went to Green Farms Academy, and I played basketball. Brian, green ball, fifteen." It stuck, and I repeated the list to him. He smiled, told me I was going to be okay, and then reminded me that no matter what happened when the doors opened, I was not to pass out under any circumstance.

The doors swung open, and chaos ensued. I don't remember a lot except dozens of people shouting, equipment swinging everywhere, and a buzzing sound near my head, which felt like there was someone pulling at it. Then, one very distinct moment: a calm man's voice saying, "Letitia, due to your injury we can't give you anything for this next part. I am so sorry, but please try not to pass out." Well, it turns out that buzzing sound was them shaving my head, and what they were about to do, with no anesthesia or numbing agents of any kind, was to staple my head shut. With each loud clamp I bit down on the towel they gave me to muffle my screams, and all I could think of was my kids and not passing out. Somehow I knew that if I passed out, I would not come back. There had to be more to my life than this. My kids needed their mom; I could not give in or up.

Thanks to the efforts of the emergency response teams, I survived the accident. Steve and the kids eventually showed up. That mysterious ambulance guy came back when no one was in the room and asked me if I remembered what I was supposed to tell him. I said, "Brian, green ball, fifteen." He smiled, nodded, and left. The strange thing is, no one ever saw him but me. In fact, according to the report, there were two men in the back of that ambulance with me, and neither was some huge white guy. No one in the ER saw him, and there is no record of him anywhere. All I know is he helped save my life, he made me fight, and he gave me my memory back.

What would come next was a far greater nightmare than the accident itself. I would endure months of headaches, seizures, vertigo, panic attacks, emotional outbursts, suicidal thoughts, and so much more. But even with the damage wrought by this landmine, I would regain all of my abilities and in eight months have a full recovery. But I couldn't wait that long to return to auctioneering.

Taking the Stage with Post-Concussive Syndrome and PTSD

Taking the stage after my accident was a huge risk, one that came with consequences as well as rewards. As my hairstylist for life will tell you, just days after it happened, I ventured into the salon a complete mess. She had to shave parts of my scalp, avoid staples, and make me look some semblance of beautiful for my next event. There was no time for feeling sorry for myself. I needed to get back out on the stage.

On the fifth of December, only eight days after the accident, I performed at the ICAN fundraising event for at-risk youth in the East Valley. There were only about 200 people in a ballroom for this event, but even still my head was spinning from the crowd, the noise, the painkillers, and most especially, the lights. I pushed my brain far too hard by trying to perform from memory. Honestly, I have barely any recollections of this auction at all, let alone the Red Brunch event I would do the next morning and hemorrhage backstage and still perform. I had convinced myself that I was ready to return to the stage, but really, the greater risk—likely with a better end result— would have been for me to rest and take care of myself before returning full-throttle to work.

Then, on December 13, I had my final event of the year: Alice Cooper's Christmas Pudding. That year it took place at Comerica Theatre, which seats about 5,000 people. The previous year, I had met Johnny Depp there. I had worn a beautiful long gown and had long blonde hair. This year, I showed up in a short Versace dress with very short hair and a hair piece covering the patches of shaved scalp, and I recall seeing the executive director's face drop when he caught sight of me. He tried to cover up his initial shock, but it was hard to disguise: beyond the new hairdo, the stress from the accident had aged me about ten years, and everyone noticed it.

When I got onstage, I picked a point in the room to focus on and lightly used my fingers to balance myself. I felt like it was 2:00 A.M. and the vodka bottle was empty, but as long as I maintained my gaze on that predetermined point in the crowd and anchored myself with my fingers, I was able to keep everything straight enough to avoid passing out—and still do a good job.

Passion, dedication, and the stubbornness of a mule kept me going until I could find my balance again.

However, even passion and persistence couldn't prevent my head trauma from taking its toll. When they flushed me with the white lights onstage, I became disoriented. For a moment in time, I didn't know where I was. It was the first time that had happened, but it wouldn't be the last. I maintained my composure and made it through the experience, but after that night I began to experience bouts of light-triggered disorientation, as well as seizures and vertigo. I could be driving on a highway and suddenly not know where I was, and I would have to pull off the road and regroup before I could continue onward. White lights became a huge trigger for my post-traumatic stress disorder as well, which is unfortunate when your job requires you to be in the spotlight.

Cue the *Rocky* theme song.

But I refused to let my accident hold me back from my passion. I could have called it quits right then and there and let fear dictate my destiny. I could have never performed at another auction again and allowed my PTSD to set a reserve on my life. While there were negative consequences of getting back onstage too soon (as can happen with any risk you take), ultimately my persistence was well founded. Not only was I able to continue building the career I love, but I was forced to work harder to cultivate balance in my life, something that previously had been lacking and that would be crucial for me as I encountered the next set of landmines that lay ahead.

Don't Let the Landmines Control Your Focus

Just like in the game "Roses and Thorns," it is crucial that you identify potential opportunities—even those hidden among the thorns or landmines. If you let the landmines distract you from the roses that are in store for you, then you'll never get to where you want to be.

Yes, it's scary to get back out there after being knocked down, whether figuratively or literally, as in my case. But if you focus on the chance of confronting another obstacle, you'll take your vision off the place where it needs to be—laser-focused on your main goal, your core intention. There are greater rewards in store for those who don't tiptoe around risks and instead run fearlessly after their dreams. Remember, setting that reserve on your life inhibits your success by limiting your opportunities. You need to look up, look around, and not let fears or self-limiting beliefs divert you from your target.

There are greater rewards in store for those who don't tiptoe around risks and instead run fearlessly after their dreams.

Oftentimes, we—and not some cataclysmic event—are the biggest obstacle to achieving our dreams. Yes, I'm talking about imposter syndrome, a term that refers to the tendency we have to think that we are not qualified enough, not worthy enough, not whatever enough to deserve success or happiness. Our monkey brain makes excuses as to why we are not taking more risks. It convinces us that we aren't entitled to more and so we don't try to achieve more. In order to defeat your own greatest enemy, you need to shut the monkey up. It can throw crap at you all day, but it is your choice to take control and stop it from dictating your life.

I cannot tell you how many people tried to tell me I would never achieve a quarter of what I have in my life, especially after my head injury. But by sitting with the discomfort of my fear and trauma, acknowledging it while still moving forward through the landmines of life, and shifting my perspective to focus on the opportunities in the path ahead, I was always able to move beyond misery and pain into purpose and freedom.

Let's Play "Roses and Thorns"

- What are the "roses" in your life right now—the positives, the visible opportunities, the pockets of joy? What are you grateful for at this moment in time?

- What are the "thorns"—the challenges, the prickly parts of your life? Where are you struggling? What obstacles do you believe are holding you back from the life you want?

- Reframe your perspective: What opportunities can you identify within these "thorns"? How can you transform any of the negative associated with them into fuel for your success? Or is there a hidden opportunity available to you that you haven't acknowledged because you've been preoccupied with the bad?

CHAPTER 6

CHECK YOUR PERSPECTIVE

I cried because I had no shoes, then I met a man with no feet.

—Mahatma Gandhi

O nce you know your calling, you've got to get perspective in order to set out on a path that turns that vision into a reality. That is, perspective on where you are currently, where you want to be, and what is preventing you from getting there. Perspective is your perceived set of roadblocks in the way of answering your calling.

> Perspective is your perceived set of roadblocks in the way of answering your calling.

Issues vs. Problems

When I became a single mother and had to work five jobs to make ends meet, I thought I had problems. I was trying to create a good life for my children and trying to make as much money as I could. Especially when beginning my career as an auctioneer, I would complain about not having enough. I had two kids and, in my mind, no money to fund my ability to jump ship and start over. Thankfully, I ignored the voice in my head telling me that I shouldn't take a risk and pursued my new career wholeheartedly. In 2008, the total income reported on my tax return was $21,064. Less than eight years later, I had earned my place as America's foremost auctiontainer. Money never stopped me from success, but a poverty mindset might have. The times when I was focusing on my perceived difficulties, I was setting a limitation on myself, while also ignoring the blessings I had in my life. In my experience, when bombarded with challenges, it's important to distinguish between issues and problems so that every obstacle does not become a reason to restrict your potential.

> The times when I was focusing on my perceived difficulties, I was setting a limitation on myself.

So, how do you determine whether you're dealing with an issue or a problem? An issue is simply an altered state of your current reality. In other words, it can be overcome because it's temporary, it's mostly in your head, and chances are, you are allowing it far too much space and power in your mind. With an issue, you're creating an unnecessary roadblock to your success. As such, it has a pretty simple fix: it just requires a change in your perception.

A problem, on the other hand, is the upheaval of your current reality. It is finite or permanent. It requires the complete acceptance of an ending to your life as you knew it. A problem will bring a mix of feelings from grief to anxiety to anger, and it can truly overwhelm and unsettle your entire world. Confronting it requires a lot of time, love, patience, and kindness to yourself and your loved ones. Problems typically necessitate a longer journey to achieving your success; however, you *will* get there. I know, because I have been through hell and back numerous times and have come out on the other side stronger spiritually, emotionally, and even professionally.

This understanding of issues versus problems was one that I would learn on one level in my volunteer work and on an entirely other, more personal level as I was sharpened on the blade of life. After I lost my ex-husband, and then again after I lost my plus-one child, I discovered through pain what true problems are.

> An issue is an altered state of your current reality, whereas a problem is the end of your current reality.

A Trio of Heartbreaks

On July 22, 2015, I kissed my children goodbye as I headed to the airport for a work trip to Nantucket. Their father was supposed to pick them up in an hour. I was getting settled into my room at the inn when my son called me. I saw our landline number on the caller ID and froze, knowing that the kids should have been at their dad's house by then. When I picked up the phone, my son said, "Daddy never came." Something deep inside the pit of my stomach sank.

I snapped into action, making several calls to find someone to watch the kids and someone to go to Steve's house. Finally, I got a hold of Steve's brother, gave him the garage code to Steve's house, and stayed with him on the phone as he discovered Steve's body slumped over on his desk. All I could do was let out some sort of primal scream as I was told that Steve had shot himself in the head.

I was supposed to work at an auction the next night for St. Jude Children's Research Hospital, but instead I walked over to the airport, which was right across the street from the inn, at 4:00 A.M. and parked myself outside, waiting for it to open and find a flight back home. I took the first little island hopper out of there.

I cried hysterically on that short flight to Boston. As soon as the plane came to a stop, the pilot let everyone off except me, reached her hand back and put it on mine, and asked me what was wrong. After I told her what had happened, she made some calls, and the next thing I knew there was an American Airlines representative on the plane ready to escort me through the Boston airport. He said, "I'm going to walk you through the airport, and I'm just going to take you through your day." He brought me to my next gate, and then he went over to talk to the gate attendant. I'm not sure what he said, but all I know is that I was able to have an entire row of seats all to myself on that flight from Boston back to Arizona. The flight attendants never made me sit up—they just fastened the seatbelt over me as I lay in a fetal position across the seats. They treated me with the utmost kindness and sympathy, bringing me pillows and blankets and letting some of the passengers around me know what had happened.

But that was the worst plane ride of my life. I knew that as soon as I landed, I was going to have to face my kids and the reality of what had happened. As long as I was on that plane, I could be numb or drown myself in the sorrow of Steve's death, but when I arrived in Phoenix I knew that I would have to be strong for my children.

Jeff, who had since become my fiancé, had picked up the kids. When I was able to join them, we all went over to Steve's house, where we discovered that he was being evicted. Having sequestered the kids in another part of the house, Jeff and I, along with Steve's brother and his wife, cleaned up the gruesome scene and moved his belongings out before the bank repossessed it. This experience put even my accident in perspective. It was also a process that finally enabled Jeff to grieve the loss of his own brother by suicide. Even still, it proved to be too much for our relationship to take.

And the universe wasn't done with me yet.

Eventually, I was able to pull my life and my children's lives back together. After Jeff and I split up, I met and fell in love with another man named Mark. Then, tragedy struck again: three years after we lost Steve, Mark would walk into his ex-wife's garage to find his seventeen-year-old son and my beloved plus-one child dead, having died by suicide. Standing by Mark's side as he walked through the hell that is mourning the loss of a child, I released the grief of Steve's death, as Jeff had done for his brother years before. Unfortunately, Mark's profound grief tore us apart, and I was left to once again pick up the pieces of my life, emerging with a stronger sense of myself, my priorities, and the extreme gratitude with which I would infuse all my thoughts and actions.

Getting Perspective by Giving Back

I sincerely hope that you never have to experience an iota of the pain and suffering described above. But it's likely that at some point in your life, you will encounter a problem—some difficulty that changes the very fabric of your life. More often than not, though, what you will face on a regular basis are issues, not problems in the true sense of the word.

So, how do you gain perspective? It's actually pretty simple: give back.

> How do you gain perspective? It's actually pretty simple: give back.

Years before I experienced the tragedies described above, my work with nonprofits like St. Jude had recalibrated my outlook: unless you're unable to afford the basic necessities of life, a lack of money is not a problem; it's an issue—one that pales in comparison with a true problem like pediatric cancer.

One of the ways I've set myself apart in my industry is that I volunteer for every single nonprofit for which I raise money. Even before I started my career as an auctioneer, I began volunteering at Camp Rainbow every year. When I went those first years, I thought I was too old, too broke, and had way too many problems to actually succeed in my new chosen career as an auctioneer. But spending eight days with young, terminally ill children with the greatest attitudes, the most positive outlook, and the most brutal honesty I've ever encountered brought all my so-called "problems" into perfect perspective.

I was the only thing stopping me.

One event at camp in particular always reset my outlook. "A Time to Remember" is a very special opening ceremony, first conceived of by a young girl who was sad that after losing her friend to cancer, camp had gone on as usual, even though her friend was not there to enjoy it. Faced with her own mortality at a young age, she mentioned to the camp director that she hoped one day, if she were gone, someone would take the time to remember her—and so was born "A Time to Remember" at Camp Rainbow. During this event, all the children gather together in an outdoor amphitheater that we call "the sacred place," and they are invited to stand up and take time to remember their loved ones whom they have lost to cancer. It is a ceremony of tears, of laughter at happy memories—a true celebration of life—and it sets the tone for the rest of the week at camp. Then, after an intense ceremony in which the children come face to face with their own mortality by processing the loss of their friends, they rush off to engage excitedly in their camp activities. Talk about perspective: If those children could approach life in that manner, then what was stopping me? The answer to that question was *me*. I was the only thing stopping me.

The same way that there is a literal voice inside your head that draws you toward your passions, there is also a dialogue in your head that plays to your fears, deceiving you by saying that you can't do whatever it is you've set your mind on. This little voice makes you shortsighted—worse yet, it keeps you looking downward, focused on your potential fall rather than charting your journey forward. In the previous chapter, I mentioned the tendency for our focus to remain on the ground when we're in a patch of landmines. Even when we seem to be clear of these problems, we're still looking down, watching and waiting for the next explosion, while we tiptoe carefully through life. The best way to combat this tendency and to gain perspective on your issues and problems is to serve others. It allows us to look up, look outward, and expand our horizons.

Giving back to someone who truly can't help themselves will show you that yes, in fact, you *can* help yourself. You *can* rise above your issues and persevere through your problems to attain your soul's deepest desires. This has been one of the greatest secrets to my success. It is a practice in which I engage regularly and will continue to do for the rest of my life.

One of the best risks you can take is opening yourself up to a spirit of gratitude. When you do this, the universe becomes filled with opportunities rather than issues, trials instead of problems. If you don't restrict your perspective, you can find blessings in even the worst of circumstances and, by focusing on them, cultivate a joyful and peace-filled existence.

Do You Have an Issue or a Problem?

- Write a list of the challenges you are currently facing. Include ones that you think are affecting your success and/or your general happiness.

- Use this list to create a chart. Title one column "Issues" and the other one "Problems." Recognizing that issues are temporary setbacks, often ones that simply require a mental shift to overcome, whereas problems change the very nature of life as you know it, transfer the challenges from your original list into their appropriate categories.

- For each item in the "Issues" category, write one sentence that details how you can give back to gain perspective on that challenge: Where can you volunteer your time, or whose live can you add value to, in order to shift your mindset and move beyond that issue?

- Now comes the difficult part. For every item in the "Problems" category—and I hope there are few—journal about how you can work through it. Allow yourself to experience and process all the emotions, grieve the life you used to know, and make plans for what you see in your future. When you're ready, re-establish a target for the path you want your new to life to take, and go through the activities in Chapter 3 to set concrete goals to get you there.

CHAPTER 7

REACH OUT, DON'T LEAN IN

Life is like a box of crayons. Most people are the eight color boxes, but what you're really looking for are the sixty-four color boxes with the sharpeners on the back.

—John Mayer

I t's kind of a running joke among people who know me that if I hear the phrase "lean in," I cringe. This reaction has nothing to do with Sheryl Sandberg, as I admire a great deal about her accomplishments. It has everything to do with the directive itself.

When I think about the idea of leaning in, I imagine a circle and someone moving their body into the circle and away from the others around them. In a circle, there is a sense of exclusion: someone is left on the outside. When you "lean in" to this already exclusory setting, your perspective becomes even more circumscribed. You're looking inward at a select group rather than outward at a diverse crowd. Right or wrong, for me, "leaning in" conjures up images of Western settlers in a circle of covered wagons, trying to keep out danger by looking inward at each other rather than outward toward the landscape. I mean, what if these pioneers just "leaned in" when they were approached by wolves or another external threat?

All joking aside, there is a real danger there—and not to the person who is left out (who often has a broader framework for considering the scene), but more so to the person leaning in. Leaning in limits your perspective. And the further you lean in, the narrower and more finite your vantage point becomes.

Leaning in limits
your perspective.

We Need All Kinds of People in Our Network

To be sure, Sandberg's concept of "leaning in" isn't restricted to a circle, but it does entail women getting ahead in their careers by pressing inward at the dinner table, the interview, the meeting, etc. The danger comes for anyone—male or female—when you're so forward-focused that you lose a sense of what's around you. When you view your success journey as linear and, as such, necessitating perpetual movement *past* people, rather than as a series of ebbs and flows contextualized within a larger network of human beings, you close yourself off to the best opportunities for growth and success.

> When you view your success journey as linear, you close yourself off to the best opportunities for growth and success.

Allow me to give you a more concrete example. Let's take your physical and nutritional health. It is common knowledge in the world of nutrition that following a diet diverse in color equates to following a diet rich in various nutrients. If you were to come to my house for dinner on any given night, you would see an assortment of red, green, orange, and yellow colors, along with proteins, healthy carbs, vegetables, and sometimes even fruit. This wide range of colors is meant to ensure that my children and I are feeding our bodies everything they need to grow, stay strong, fight off disease, and maintain good mental and physical health. Now, if I were to prepare a single-hued plate with the same exact protein or carb over and over again, eventually we would become weak or even sick. To be thoroughly nourished, your body requires a diversity of types and colors of food. Similarly, if you don't want to set a reserve on your life, you need to open it up to a range of people with different viewpoints and experiences than your own. Doing so feeds our souls rather than our bodies, offers us unique sources of support, and strengthens us by broadening our perspective.

> If you don't want to set a reserve on your life, you need to open it up to a range of people with different viewpoints and experiences than your own.

If you lean in to a group of people who are similar in age, race, religion, interests, goals, and family dynamic to you, then you might as well just be eating one food every day for the rest of your life. It's not healthy, and it can even be destructive. This tendency is what drives the dangerous echo chambers of social media, and it's one of the main things hindering people from attaining success and finding fulfillment. Combating this tunnel vision is what brought me one of my closest friends and savior of my soul, Jennie—a woman who never would have ended up in my network had I been "leaning in."

Circle K Decaf with a Kick

I don't drink caffeinated coffee—I have plenty of zing without it!—but I really enjoy the taste, so I drink decaf. Back when I was a struggling, broke, single mother, I could no longer afford Starbucks, so I switched to Circle K's brew and their 89-cent refill Mondays. Unlike Starbucks, where the edgiest occurrence was someone misspelling my name on my cup, Circle K came with a sassy, outspoken cashier who liked to complain about her job and make off-color remarks about my choice of heels and clothing.

My day would start something like this: I would head over to the decaf, notice the carafe was empty, and mention this fact to the cashier, who is responsible for keeping it full. Her response would always start with a rather loud, "Well, if it isn't old hooker heels herself!" Of course, her strident comment would catch the other customers in the store off guard, and it reminded me I had fallen far from Starbucks's grace. She may not have asked to write my name on a cup, but she definitely caught my attention enough that I would never forget her name: Jennie.

Over time, Jennie and I got to talking, and I discovered that we had far more in common than either of us thought. Jennie had grown up in the foster care system and was raising a son alone, doing the best she could with the limited resources and education that life had dealt her. Jennie was determined to break the cycle of poverty for her boy and give him a life better than the one she knew—a task that grew a little more challenging when she became pregnant with her second son. Although I was in a more privileged position than Jennie, I was raising two children alone and knew the trials and tribulations of being a single mother working minimum-wage jobs to make ends meet.

Rather than pressing exclusively inward into the network of celebrities, business leaders, and distinguished auctioneers with whom I was regularly rubbing shoulders, I opened myself up to growth from outside the box—or circle, as it were. *I leaned out.* And when I did, my perspective was enriched, as was Jennie's, in ways that we are still benefiting from to this day.

> I opened myself up to growth from outside the circle.
> *I leaned out.*

Our friendship grew, and I ended up throwing Jennie a baby shower with several other Circle K customers and getting her everything she needed for her new baby. I went on to teach her about housesitting, walking dogs, cleaning, and other jobs that paid better than Circle K, and even helped get her older son started with free dancing at The Rock Teen Center. Jennie once said something to me in a softer moment between us about our friendship: "I just never thought a woman like you would ever bother to know a girl like me." There it is right there—she thought I would only "lean in," but instead I reached out.

Jennie and I were both single mothers, both broke financially, and both determined to get out from under our present circumstances, but we did not look the same, sound the same, or grow up in the same environment. Jennie shared a lot of wisdom about what we had in common based on what we did *not* have in common, and vice versa. Now Jennie works part-time for me helping clean my house, and we are both holding out for the day I can afford to get her that Missy Elliott track suit and black Escalade and hire her as my head of security when I hit it big. That is her vision, by the way.

In the meantime, though, she is killing it. After being part of the Phoenix Mercury dance squad at just eighteen years old, her eldest son is in now in Los Angeles dancing. Her youngest is a straight-A student and future professional athlete. Jenny is with the father of her second child, has lost over fifty pounds, has gotten her diabetes and health under control, makes more than double what she used to, and only works at Circle K one day a week. She is a better version of herself and is moving closer to the life she envisions for herself every day. She also happens to be one of my best friends, with whom I can cry, laugh, and share my deepest fears. Jennie and I have been together through thick and thin, and there is nothing I would not do for her or her children. We feed each other's soul because we reached out, not because we leaned in.

I have countless friends beyond just Jennie—in fact, you'll meet another one in the next chapter—with whom I might never have connected had I been focused on leaning in to some inner circle. There is Doug, my bestie in a wheelchair living with ALS who is making it up mountains to re-propose to his wife; Patricia, a bathroom attendant, former drug pusher, and domestic violence survivor who is now a published author and speaker; and countless others who have enriched my life beyond words. This is why I cringe when I hear the phrase "lean in"—because Sandberg unknowingly and certainly unintentionally created a trend of women leaning in to other women who look, sound, act, and think like each other, when in truth, we should be reaching out to one another, male and female, adding variety to our lives and nourishing the diet of our soul.

Are You Leaning In or Reaching Out?

- Imagine yourself seated at a table with everyone you consider to be in your "network." Who is at that table with you?

- Out of this list of people, do you think you have enough variety at the table? If you had to assign everyone at the table a color based on their personality, history, experience, and other unique qualities, would you have a rainbow or a monochromatic meal? Is there a diversity of perspectives in your network or is it just another echo chamber?

- What sort of perspectives would you benefit from adding to your network? How do you imagine them contributing to your success and happiness? How can you reach out to gain these additional viewpoints?

CHAPTER 8

IT TAKES ONLY ONE

A mentor is someone who allows you to see the hope inside yourself.

—Oprah Winfrey

"I knew it was going to be okay as soon as you believed in me." I hear this refrain frequently from my numerous mentees in and beyond the auction industry.

The problem is, that attitude is a complete catch-22.

My belief in them is not really what matters. What matters is that when they perceived I believed in them, they then believed in themselves. However, waiting for someone else's acknowledgment of your value is a set-up for failure. It prevents you from taking ownership of your life and gifts until you get that external validation. Waiting is like setting a huge reserve on your life. It limits the reach of your talents. It limits your success. And it limits the lives you will touch.

You've heard that old adage that "It takes only one"—and that's absolutely true. However, no one explains to us that *the one is you*. We have to arrange our life so that we are able to be the one for ourselves.

> It only takes one, and the one is *you*. You are your own greatest mentor.

People are always looking for someone to help them up, but that upward focus is all wrong. Rather than searching for someone who will develop our talents, we should be developing them ourselves by finding ways to share our gifts. Don't get me wrong, mentors are invaluable sources of strength, but relying on one to help us before we will take action shifts the accountability into someone else's domain. The greatest mentors will teach you that *you alone* already have within you what it takes to succeed: you are, and will always be, your own greatest mentor.

It's Not Mine

I have been very blessed with some impactful mentors like Foster Friess, who arrived in my life at the right moment with a perspective that helped me break through my limitations. I first met Foster and his wife Lynn at a backyard auction. I had gone to Haiti to volunteer with one of my clients, and she organized the event upon our return. When it came time for the ask, Foster and Lynn ended up matching the amount of approximately $285,000. I watched them as they stood up, amazed by their effortless generosity. After giving away that much money, they were giggling and holding hands like teenagers out on a first date. I was completely bewildered by their happiness and ease.

At the time of this backyard auction, I had not yet encountered the major problems in my life like my accident and the deaths of loved ones that would follow, but I was not really out of the woods from having financial problems. So I found Foster, and I asked him about his attitude of generosity. With a chuckle, he said, "Do you want to know a secret?"

I waited, ready to receive the holy grail—some profound, life-changing insight. And it was. It just wasn't what or how I expected.

He continued, "It's not our money."

At this point, I'm thinking, "What? What do you mean it's not your money? Whose is it then?"

And he whispers, very simply, "It's not our money. It's God's. We were just charged with giving it away."

I pressed further and asked, "What do you mean?"

"Everyone's been blessed with something, Letitia. We just happen to have been blessed with the good fortune to have done our business right. We've been given the obligation and the honor of giving away God's money. What have you been given?"

As I left the event, I reflected, "Well, only wealthy people give away money. Only wealthy people leave the sort of legacy that you are leaving through your donations. People like me don't have anything like that to offer."

But I couldn't get Foster's words out of my head. As I sat in my car that night, I wondered, "What does he mean? What did God give me?"

> I don't need hundreds of millions of dollars to give away what God has given me to share.

Then it dawned on me: He gave me talent—*and it's not mine.* I don't need hundreds of millions of dollars to give away what God has given me to share. I already have it. Foster helped me understand that I have something to give. Not only did this enhance my own sense of value, but it made me realize that I was only scratching the surface with the mentoring relationships I had already begun. After this, I began to mentor other female auctioneers regularly, and unlike pretty much anyone in this industry I have never taken referral fees or charged for my instruction. I view my talent as a gift that I am tasked with sharing to help change others' lives and, by extension, the lives of the people they serve.

Although Foster would end up being a long-time mentor for me, he also taught me that mentoring others is far more important than finding a mentor yourself. In reality, the people we end up mentoring will become our greatest mentors.

> Our greatest mentors will be the people we mentor.

Your Fantastic Five

According to Jim Rohn, you are the average of the five people with whom you spend the most time. I believe there are some large gaps and presumptions in that statement. The largest is the underlying WIIFM (What's In It For Me) in these relationships: "If I surround myself only with millionaires, then I can drain them of their knowledge and wisdom and join their club." But as I learned from Foster Friess, the greatest mentor in your life should be you. You need to ask yourself, how are you helping others succeed and exceed what you have accomplished?

> How are you helping others succeed and exceed what you have accomplished?

I teach others what I have learned from not only building a career in the auction industry, but also serving as a trailblazer who developed the genre of "auctiontaining." In my role as a mentor, I support others free of charge as they work to become brilliant and successful auctioneers. Not everything has to be about money, but it should always be about helping others pull themselves up.

Rather than focusing on the five people in your network after whom you are trying to mold your life, consider that your success is determined by those five people whom you have helped to become successful. Channel your energies into five (or more) people whose lives you can positively impact. Remember that core message I emphasize throughout this book: giving is the central strategy for success. Regardless of how much or how little you think you have to offer, it's going to be valuable to someone somewhere. Open yourself up to opportunities to give back and you'll be amazed at where you—and your mentees—will end up. The more you help, the greater your success will be. It has a reciprocal effect in the universe, as nature abhors a vacuum. When you create light in other people's lives, the universe is obligated to bless your life.

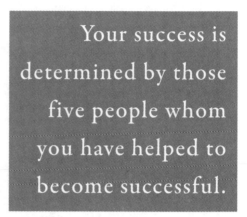

> Your success is determined by those five people whom you have helped to become successful.

But you have to be accountable to yourself and to those whom you guide. Keeping your word is important, and it is doubly so for those you mentor and those who mentor you. No one likes smoke blown up their keister. If someone offers you help, you must uphold your end of the bargain, and vice versa. When mentoring someone, you have to see them through to the end. You must be available to support them when they need you, not when it is convenient for you.

There is a great reward for those who focus on mentoring rather than being mentored. For one thing, surrounding yourself with people who are passionate can be infectious. This is why I am so empowered and energized by children battling illnesses. They don't want to merely survive; they want to *live*. That passion is inspirational and, at times, overwhelming. They make me want to be a better person, to live my life to its fullest. I then transfer that passion into each auction I do in their honor. That's the secret sauce that loosens people's hearts and opens their wallets. The children's passion, combined with the energy from the auction, gives those in attendance permission to be warriors for change; and so, offering their money becomes easy for them. It begins with the flame of passion that turns into a fire—a fire that I am fortunate enough to be able to translate to others.

> It is through action and application that theory gets refined into strategies.

Another benefit of mentoring others is how much more effectively you learn as a teacher than as a student. Oftentimes it takes application to understand fully the principles we preach. Through my mentees I've come to truly understand, by witnessing firsthand, the importance of having a concrete vision, of distinguishing between issues and problems, of drawing on your sources of strength. Before these ideas are implemented in your own life as well as the lives of those with whom we're working, they are pure theory; it is through action and application that they get refined into strategies.

Again resisting the urge to lean in, I reach out instead: Who can I mentor in order to help them become aligned with their passion, create the life they want, and, most importantly, help others along the way?

Get Real and Get Going

One of my first mentees was a woman named Tamara, whom I met early in my career. At the time, I was doing $100-a-day auctions at a warehouse, where she worked as a forklift driver. Tamara had a wonderful presence to her and a certain beauty, despite the fact that she was missing most of her teeth. She worked in the warehouse all week, preparing for the auction day by loading and unloading pallets of items and cataloging thousands of miscellaneous items. She, like me at the time, was living under or close to the poverty line while raising two little kids.

I bumped into Tamara some three or four years after I left that job and was well on my way in my current career. I was in the warehouse, not as an auctioneer, but rather as a teacher in an auction school being held there. I was done for the day and was heading out when Tamara came running up to hug me. She had tears in her eyes and told me how much she loved following me on social media and how deeply she wanted to be a part of my industry and to help others through her work. We shared a moment of total sincerity, where I could see in her eyes how much she meant every word she said. She told me that she could feel destiny literally pulling at her and that she had a vision of a life that involved giving back to others. It was obvious to me that Tamara knew that she was meant for more and was willing to do the work to get there.

I decided to ask her out to lunch the following week to talk with her about her vision. Now, to say that Tamara and I looked like an odd pair to be dining out together is an understatement, a fact that did not slip past our waiter as he continuously, and very rudely, kept staring at Tamara as if he were going to throw her out. She came straight from the warehouse covered in dirt, missing all but a few teeth, and reeking of cigarette smoke. I was wearing a dress with designer heels, having just come from a day of meetings with clients. Let's just say that there was no one in that restaurant looking at us and assuming we were in some sort of "leaning in" circle together.

The truth is we were a lot alike. It was not all that long ago that I was living at the poverty line and had trouble putting food on the table for my kids. I saw myself in Tamara, and I saw nothing but pure passion and drive. Using the approach to goal-setting discussed in Chapter 3, I told Tamara to describe what she visualized in her life and asked her my famous question: "What do you truly want?" Tamara was able to describe her life in full detail: she pictured herself going into all sorts of fancy ballrooms, being around celebrities and wealthy bidders, and helping raise money for others in need. In fact, she had her vision down to a T—she could literally see it; she just could not understand how to get it. I decided to begin the journey of reaching out and mentoring her, but first I needed to know if Tamara was aware of something.

I am a very blunt person. With me, what you see is what you get, so don't be surprised at this next part. After Tamara painted this beautiful vision of her ideal life, I hit her with a cold reality. I asked her a question: "Do you see famous leaders, celebrities, or business icons you admire chain smoking?" Tamara had been smoking over two packs of cigarettes a day for years, probably since she was about thirteen, and now she was around forty. Her answer was "No." I needed to know if Tamara could be honest about things in her current life that might be preventing her from activating that vision of her ideal life. You see, writing down your vision and bringing intention into your life is imperative, but so is acknowledging anything you are currently doing that flies directly counter to that. As long as Tamara could see that about herself, I knew she could do something about it herself, and for that, I was all in.

After hearing the candor in Tamara's response, I agreed to mentor her, and we started with exactly what I have described before—a journal to write down what had previously been visions seen only inside her head. She needed to focus them and give them intention. Well, Tamara did just that. After almost twenty years of chain smoking, Tamara quit and has never gone back. If you have ever known someone who smokes, especially someone who has a two-pack-a-day habit, you know that is no easy task. Yet Tamara did it. In her journal, she wrote about having a beautiful smile with healthy teeth. The funny thing is, just a few weeks after we started our mentor-mentee relationship I got a call from a well-known dentist who specializes in dental care for underprivileged children and their families asking if I would consult with him on fundraising for his new inner-city project. What are the chances, right? I had someone in my life who needed new teeth, and along came an opportunity to exchange my services for her vision, the vision she had written down just a few weeks earlier. The universe sends blows, but it also sends grace in abundance.

> The universe sends blows, but it also sends grace in abundance.

Tamara now has a beautiful smile, went on to receive a scholarship to an auction school, took computer classes, and yes, works with me in every ballroom of every size with every celebrity and donor raising money for those in need—and not only for me, but also for national car auctions, estate sales, and some of the biggest names in celebrity charity auctions. Along the way, Tamara also moved from the forklift to the office and is now the executive assistant in the largest female-owned logistics firm in Arizona, all part of the vision she once wrote down. I invested my time and energy into Tamara before I had "made it"—before I was at a point in my career when people actively sought me out as a mentor—and it helped her achieve her dreams. I, in turn, received the satisfaction of witnessing her success journey and benefiting

132

from her friendship and support. I took the reserve off my ability to give and received dividends beyond belief.

> I took the reserve off my ability to give and received dividends beyond belief.

Why Aren't You Going All In?

Most people in the world want to leave some sort of legacy. And typically, when we think of a legacy, we think of a physical building, a scholarship in our name, or some other tangible, money-driven item. These are all wonderful endeavors and goals toward which every one of us should be working, but the pressure to have wealth or status in order to exercise our generosity often limits our giving.

Because of this tendency, I like to distinguish between a legacy and an impression. Whereas a legacy is the tangible sign of material success, an impression is a stamp of sincerity left on someone's soul—often one that motivates them to act.

> Whereas a legacy is the tangible sign of material success, an impression is a stamp of sincerity left on someone's soul.

Many people believe that impressions are fleeting and, therefore, not worth investing time and energy into, but exactly the opposite is true. The English word *impression* comes from the Latin word *imprimere*, which means "to press into or upon" or "to stamp." Think of a footprint: a footprint leaves an impression on the ground of the person walking. The person departs, but the footprint is left as a sign of the person having walked there. It is a note written into the landscape signifying that the person took action in that space. Similarly, when you leave an impression on another person, you make a mark on their life, creating positive change that outlasts your interaction with them.

Consider people like Gandhi and Mother Teresa. They lacked material riches, but still they touched the lives of so many. They left impressions on people and, by extension, the world. They did not use an absence of wealth as an excuse to withhold their generosity. Instead, they exercised it in abundance: they gave back, they kept their word, and they believed in themselves, which allowed them to believe in other people. They were consistent, and they were accountable—the two most important characteristics of a mentor. Their lives teach us that impressions outlast buildings, plaques, and other pawns of time. Instead, they move the needle of humanity toward the common good.

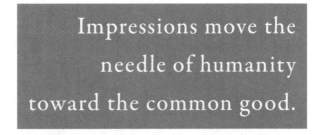

Impressions move the needle of humanity toward the common good.

Why aren't more of us striving to leave an impression? My "aha" moment in this regard occurred when I was touring the Barrow Neurological Institute in Phoenix, Arizona. One of the amazing aspects of my job is that I get to serve as the link between donor and recipient: as an auctioneer, I connect with the donors at the fundraising events, but I also tour the organizations for which I'm raising money, enabling me to translate the passion and the purpose into the auctions I lead. So when I was invited to tour Barrow, I jumped at the opportunity. I was able to spend the day with ALS patients and get a behind-the-scenes look at the facility, and it caused me to reflect and recognize that I wanted to make an impression—I wanted to do something that would leave a mark and encourage other people to act as well. I gained clarity, realizing that *legacies are things you walk into; impressions change your movement.* I made a commitment to myself not to let opportunities to leave impressions pass me by. I decided then and there to donate my brain and spinal fluid to ALS research, so now, when I die, even though I don't have ALS, those parts of my body will be transported to Barrow to help find a cure for the disease. I'm taking the front seat to my life because I choose to. There's no reserve on my life. I'm all in.

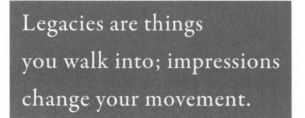

Legacies are things you walk into; impressions change your movement.

So many people are sitting in the back seat of their own life. Why? There are jobs and opportunities all over the world; you have to be willing to go after them. If this is something with which you struggle, ask yourself, *Why aren't you going all in? Why are you setting a reserve on your life?*

We all have something to give. What did God bless you with that you can give to others? Stop waiting for success, wealth, or satisfaction before you're willing to share your talents. If you give when you think you have nothing—if you offer what time, money, and/or skills you have right now, in this moment—you can leave an impression on the world and yes, even move the needle of humanity.

Are You All In?

- What opportunities to give are you missing out on because you don't think you are worthy or have anything to give? What is holding you back from going all in on the life you want?

- What are your gifts? Do you have a unique skill set? A talent? A passion for something that has made you knowledgeable about it?

- With whom could you share your talents, skills, and blessings? List five people who would benefit from these gifts. Then, make a plan for reaching out to them.

- Create a chart with two columns, one designated "Legacy" and one marked "Impressions." In the column labeled "Legacy," describe how you would like to contribute to the world materially: What financial or physical gifts do you dream of leaving behind to better your family, your community, your country, or the larger world? In the column labeled "Impressions," list ways in which you could move the needle of humanity by impacting people's lives in an intangible way—through acts of love, kindness, and service.

Why aren't you going all in?

CHAPTER 9

LIVE LIFE
IN BALANCE

Never get so busy making a living that *you forget to make a life.*

—Dolly Parton

L iving life out of balance is like riding on a carousel. You're spinning around and around, lacking an external frame of reference to key you in to how fast you are going. Any attempt to resist the ride's momentum proves incredibly hard: seemingly without rhyme or reason, you just keep going, propelled onward by the habits or behaviors on which you have come to rely. When it finally stops, you falter as you attempt to climb off, dizzy and wobbly-legged from the incessant motion. As you walk away and see the carousel in perspective, you realize that you've just been spinning in circles rather than moving forward to a new destination. You've experienced a lot of headache just to end up right where you started.

> Living an unbalanced life is like riding on a carousel: you experience a lot of headache just to end up right where you started.

When I was advancing my career, balance was completely out of the question. Every Saturday I was doing auctions for almost twelve hours. Then I began averaging about four to five charity auctions a week on top of that. I was working my retail job, taking occasional modeling gigs, and subbing for the morning traffic girl on the local news station—all of this while raising two children as a single parent. I would move from one job to the next, from work to family, without ever stopping. Of course, a large part of this chaos emerged out of necessity, because I had to put food on the table, but nonetheless it was unhealthy—and perhaps, in some ways, even limiting. Sometimes the bigger risk comes not from juggling multiple balls simultaneously, but from forcing yourself to pause the act, regroup, and learn to work with less. Because when you take that time to rebalance your responsibilities, you can lose your momentum and drop everything all at once. But remember, without risk comes little hope for reward.

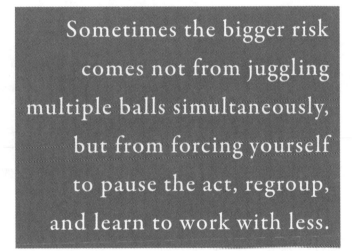

Sometimes the bigger risk comes not from juggling multiple balls simultaneously, but from forcing yourself to pause the act, regroup, and learn to work with less.

The lack of balance between the domains of work and home seeped into other areas of my life as well. I pushed the limits with almost everything: I lacked balance in my mentoring, my parenting, my romantic relationship, my sleep, and my nutrition. I began to drink wine almost every night of the week. I started relying on sedatives in order to sleep. I was running an insane number of miles each week. All of this together was priming me for burnout, which I might have experienced eventually, had I not been faced with the traumatic brain injury first. As I mention in Chapter 5, although this was a landmine in my path, it brought about the rose of perspective: I finally realized that I needed balance.

Getting off the Carousel

Unfortunately, it wasn't until some damage had been done that I accepted this lesson from the universe. Returning to the stage too quickly after my accident proved disastrous to my health: in addition to experiencing vertigo and PTSD from white lights, I began having seizures, likely from pushing myself too hard instead of allowing my brain to heal. I just could not quit, but I was really concerned about where my life was going. The doctor was handing me all types of very addictive pain medication. It felt as though my life was slipping away, and the drugs were making the slip that much easier.

I remember being at an event and talking to director and producer Tom Shadyac backstage about my struggles with dizziness and balance. He asked me a question that upended my world. He said, "Tish, I have a question for you: What was taken from you in the accident? Tell me in one word."

I responded, "Balance."

What Tom said next was revelatory for me: "Get your balance. Get your life back."

I had to admit that I was not living a balanced life. I was so focused on my career and being independent that I had lost sight of the things in life that really mattered. I was fighting a good fight; I was just fighting for the wrong things. I thought I wanted the life I had lost, when that life was totally out of balance to begin with. Sure, it was full of comfort—decadent meals, luxurious trips, and a sense that I could have anything I wanted—but the price to my soul was huge.

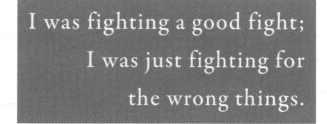

I was fighting a good fight; I was just fighting for the wrong things.

The side effects from my traumatic brain injury forced me to acknowledge, not my limits—that's the wrong way of looking at it—but rather the areas in which I needed to be more accountable to myself and to others. It's not a restriction to say that you cannot commit endless hours to work, service, or something else. When you establish a solid framework for evaluating and accepting responsibilities (aside from those that are truly forced upon you from external circumstances), you are liberating yourself to give more—to be more present, to be more available, and to share more of yourself. That freedom opens you up to a life of balance, progress, and growth, not only in terms of your career and passions, but also in terms of your relationship with yourself and with others.

Committing to Balance

Balance is not something with which we are born. It is learned through trial and error, from venturing out in different directions; identifying when things have become hectic, unhealthy, and/or disproportionate; and then realigning our endeavors with our goals. But most of all, it is honed through effort and commitment. Balance is just as much about accountability as it is stability.

> Balance is just as much about accountability as it is stability.

In my life, this has taken the form of regularly committing to wellness. I actually have a calendar at home, and every Sunday night I create my plan for balance that week. This includes marking out the days that I will drink wine, the days that I will exercise, the days that I will make a big family dinner, etc. It might sound like overplanning, but it's an important practice that has helped me recommit to living a balanced life every single week.

What's more, it's enabled me to become a more peaceful and present person. I don't have to worry about whether I should or should not be indulging at the twenty-first birthday party for one of my mentees—if it's not a scheduled wine night, I'm the designated driver. Or, in another example, if I'm asked on short notice to volunteer at an event, whereas before I might have overcommitted myself and said "yes" even if I hadn't spent enough time with my family that week, now I'm able to check my calendar and see whether it falls on a designated family night. By establishing in advance how I will practice self-care and spend time with my family while also pressing forward in my career and volunteer efforts, I am able to be accountable to myself, to my well-being, to my clients, and to my family. And remember, accountability and consistency are the hallmarks of a life well lived, one that most certainly will leave a lasting impression on the world.

In the aftermath of the accident, as I coped with seizures, vertigo, and severe anxiety, I discovered that the real treatment needed to be directed to my life, not my physical symptoms. I used passion and perspective to help me see my life and create a plan that took into account my wellness priorities—a healthy mind, body, and spirit. I began to feed these aspects of my life healthy things, and something, dare I say, miraculous happened. My dizziness went away, I regained control of my body, and I no longer felt like I was teetering all the time. This was not some fad diet or guru prescription; it was a complete lifestyle change. And it was not only my body that became more aligned; it was my entire life—my career, my family, and my purpose all began working together in harmony.

Being in balance does not make your life trouble-proof, but it does prepare you to handle the landmines when they come your way. When I received the news that the father of my children was dead, I slid back to that place of darkness and imbalance, and my physical symptoms returned. Because I recognized it and knew how to work through it, I was able to be an anchor for my children and continue to work and accelerate my career. Was I sad—depressed, even? Absolutely, but it did not have the hold over my life that it once did. I was finally off the carousel, and nothing was going to take that steady perspective away from me.

How Can You Cultivate Balance in Your Life?

- What are the areas in your life in which you feel drained, overworked, burned out, or dispassionate? What parts of your life feel chaotic, rushed, and frenzied? How are these areas characterized by imbalance?

- Are there any physical symptoms you are experiencing that might be the result of living life out of balance? Explain. In addition to seeking medical treatment, what can you do to protect and enhance your wellness?

- Buy a calendar, and on every Sunday make a game plan for the week ahead. Attending to the areas in which you struggle to maintain a balance, give items related to that area their own time slot on the calendar. Stick to this plan no matter what—be accountable to yourself. On the following Sunday, review the week's results and schedule your balanced routine for the next week.

CHAPTER 10

ACTIVATE YOUR SOURCES OF STRENGTH

Forget your perfect offering. There is a crack, a crack in everything. That's how the light gets in.

—Leonard Cohen

E very practice I share in this book essentially comes back to the same thing: your soul. When we enrich and feed our soul, we feel alive, we are focused with intention on our goals, we attract all that we need into our lives, and we become the best version of ourselves. So what happens when we get off track or are derailed from the life that we envision? I know I am not alone in knowing what it feels like to be on top of the world one second and in the gutter the next. How many times have you felt on fire, with a surplus of motivation and inspiration to achieve your dreams, only to encounter a person or situation that deflates you like a balloon? It can not only veer you off-course, but it can overhaul your vision for your life. That's when you need to utilize SOS.

A lot of people believe that SOS is an acronym that stands for "save our ship." It was indeed a distress signal sent out in Morse code by sailors when their ship was in danger of sinking. However, few people know that what it actually stands for is "save our souls." When you get off track and start losing your vison and intention, you are losing touch with your soul, so I am going to share with you something I learned about how to get back on track and into the flow of life as you see it—a way to literally cry out for help and save your soul, before your ship goes down.

Sending out a Call

As with most of the success strategies detailed in this book, I learned this one while in the service of others. People who generously give of themselves will always find that they receive far more than is required of them. I learned the practice of SOS while volunteering at a camp, this time for LGBTQ youth. Incredibly, this camp was held in the very same place as Camp

Rainbow. Everything in life comes full circle if we have the perspective to see it.

At Camp OUTdoors!, many of the youth are what I call "throwaways," not runaways. They have been kicked out of their homes due to their sexual orientation, many as young as twelve or thirteen years old, and are left to fend for themselves on the streets. As you can imagine might happen when they're made to feel so unwanted, many of the youth have thought about ending their lives. The team that runs this camp are with an organization called One-n-ten, one of my clients for over a decade now. This nonprofit actively combats the suicide rates in LGBTQ youth and young adults by providing resources to promote self-expression, empowerment, and healthy choices, a cause that touches me at a soul level having lost my plus-one child Aksel that way.

> Everything in life comes full circle if we have the perspective to see it.

Camp OUTdoors! teaches the principle of SOS, which in their programming stands for "sources of strength." The campers are taught that if and when they find themselves slipping into depression or succumbing to suicidal thoughts, they need to send out a cry for help and identify a source of strength that will help them get back on track. They "save their souls" by locating a support system that will build them up and enable them to navigate life's rocky terrain. This support system might take the form of a loving parent, an understanding friend, a self-care routine, a hobby, or some other activity, person, or pet—whatever will help them see their purpose and value and return to living their best life. Their SOS is a signal to the world that they are in distress and need help to heal, but it is also a sign to themselves: it's a reminder that they need to activate their support system to feed their soul and realign themselves with their vision and intentions.

> Activate your support system to realign yourself with your vision and intentions.

Sparking Your Soul

When I lost my ex-husband and then again my plus-one child Aksel, I went through very dark periods and had to use my SOS. For me, these sources of strength have tended to be actions or activities rather than people, though the women in my network like Jennie certainly build me back up when I'm in a low period. My SOS usually involves at least one of the following: running, spending time with my kids, being in nature, focusing on the sound of the ocean waves, cooking, listening to Joss Stone on Pandora, relaxing with my dogs, watching Will Ferrell movies or dog videos on YouTube, viewing a sunset, lighting candles, and giving back. Whenever I recognize that I am starting sink into negativity, sadness, or fear, I take a timeout and turn to my SOS. Doing this gives me the mental space and spiritual restoration I need to gain perspective and get back out there.

The key with this practice is being able to identify when you need to activate your SOS. It's harder to recognize when you're sinking emotionally than it is to realize you're going underwater in a ship. How can you catch yourself in time and send out your distress signal before you get too far off track?

One way is to establish regular check-in times with yourself, when you journal about the emotions you are experiencing and then evaluate your perspective. If it seems like there are more problems than issues and if the emotions associated with these problems (or even issues) seem too overwhelming, where you struggle even to write about them—or if you notice that your general tone is negative, self-critical, and hopeless—then you know it's time for your SOS.

Sometimes it helps to get space from what you write in your journal before assessing it for signs of distress. In that case, you might want to dedicate time every Friday night to getting everything down on paper and then reread what you wrote the next morning over coffee. In the fresh light of dawn, it might be easier to see that you're falling into despair by the day's end and, as such, need to implement some recovery strategies.

Another means of cultivating an awareness of your soul's needs is by attending to the times of day, or even the days of the week, when you tend to feel lower or more drained and then weaving your SOS into the fabric of your day. If you've identified your sources of strength, then you can build them into your daily routine and keep yourself afloat even when the metaphorical waters get choppy. That is why I make sure to schedule runs into my weekly planner and often select times that I know will be periods of high stress. I know that by running, I'll be better able to manage the challenges and my stress levels.

Here's another example: I know that there are certain songs that can instantly turn the tide in my favor—for instance, the theme to the movie *Rocky*, which is why I have made it the ringtone on my cell phone. That tune kicks me into an "I can do this" mindset in a split second. I've programmed that SOS into my day to protect myself against any unexpected lows.

Those are just two of my many sources of strength—the people, places, sounds, and actions I can turn to with little to no effort that instantly speak to my soul and redirect my mind into that arrow of intention heading straight toward its mark.

The more you practice SOS, the easier and more effective it becomes. In fact, while writing this very chapter yesterday my computer froze, leaving me wildly frustrated and a bit depressed because with my schedule, blocking out six-plus hours to write is not easy. I was in the flow of writing and suddenly everything crashed and I had to stop. Rather than give up after frantically trying to reboot my computer for two hours, I simply turned it off and hit the gym and worked out for an hour. By the time I was done, I felt completely alive and motivated, so I thought I might give it another try. As it turns out, it worked, and I was able to write until 1:30 A.M. I slept like a baby and woke up refreshed and ready to get back to it. That is just a small example. My point is this: it is crucial that you know not only how to feed and nourish your soul, but also how to save it. Keep your intentions, travel toward the life you actively envision, become the best version of yourself, and when you feel you are about to sink, activate your SOS.

Never Not Broken

The Hindu goddess Akhilandeshvari is the goddess of heartbreak, soul sickness, and transition. Her name means "never not broken," which describes her perfectly because she exists in a perpetually fragmented state: she is constantly piecing herself back together, only to tear herself apart again and reshape herself the second she finds some sort of stasis. You might think that this is some type of punishment, like Sisyphus with his boulder that he has to roll uphill for all eternity, but that's not the case. Despite her constant state of flux, the goddess's face suggests an internal state of serenity and enlightenment. Her wisdom comes from understanding that wholeness is an elusive concept and that the greatest power on earth lies in our ability to find value in our brokenness and our willingness to strengthen ourselves as we continuously refashion who we are. We can achieve this enlightenment too, if we learn to grow in and through our brokenness.

> The greatest power on earth lies in our ability to find value in our brokenness.

SOS is not a strategy meant to force you to merely "get over" your heartache, ignore your emotions, or minimize your difficulties. Rather, it's intended to help you nourish your soul as you work through challenges. Growth requires brokenness. It requires you to accept the messiness of rebuilding your life—of continually reshaping who you are—so that you can create new experiences and associations and cultivate a deeper understanding of and appreciation for your soul. Any seeming "failure," issue, or problem must be viewed as another opportunity for rebirth—for forming a kinder, wiser, and more generous version of yourself. Rather than fighting against the messiness of life, we need to use it to find our strength and power. When you finally are able to embrace your authentic self and share the fruits of your brokenness and transformation with the world, then you are truly living a live with *no reserve*.

What's Your SOS Plan?

- What are your sources of strength? What things immediately set you back into a great space mentally? Write them down. Remember that they have to be easy, because when you are in a dark place or are thrown off your game, you are not thinking clearly, so you need to be able to go to your SOS relatively mindlessly, with little to no effort.

- Set aside a night for journaling about your perspective on the past week and the week ahead. You might choose a Friday night, since we earmarked Sunday night for planning and recommitting to balance. Don't read what you wrote until the next day, preferably in the morning or at a time in your day when you think that you have the most perspective: With this new vantage point, are you able to recognize pockets of negativity, hopelessness, or frustration that need to be addressed with the SOS strategy?

- How can you program SOS into your daily and/or weekly routine? Using the list you wrote for the first question, identify three ways that you can plug your sources of strength into your regular activities so that you have an automatic system of support to build you up.

CHAPTER 11

COMMIT TO YOURSELF

Love recognizes no barriers. It jumps hurdles, leaps fences, penetrates walls to arrive at its destination full of hope.

—Maya Angelou

You've just encountered ten strategies that will help you remove the reserve from your life and open yourself up to unlimited joy, success, and generosity. These principles will enable you not only to transform your life for the better, but also to make impressions on the lives of others, moving the needle of humanity toward the greater good. But how do you ensure that you maintain your absolute life? How do you keep off the reserve in good times and in bad?

After facing a series of life-altering events—my traumatic brain injury, the death of my ex-husband, the end of my engagement, and the death of my plus-one child—I recognized that my life had been through a metamorphosis. I wanted to celebrate my inner Akhilandeshvari, my inner goddess of "never not broken." I wanted to commit to myself to use the continual fragmentation and rebuilding inherent in life as an opportunity for perpetual and unrestricted growth. I knew that I needed something to commemorate my promise to myself to live an absolute life and to serve as a reminder that I had made this commitment when challenges arose.

On November 21, 2018, I invited a group of friends, my two children, and my then-boyfriend Mark to Mountain Shadows Resort in Paradise Valley, Arizona. My friends had no idea why I had gathered them together, so it was a complete shock to them when they attended a ceremony in which I married myself, in essence.

Mark walked me down the aisle and gave me away, as my daughter sang a gorgeous rendition of "La Vie en rose." My son had been ordained to conduct the wedding ceremony, and my good friend had made a stunning diamond eternity band to mark the occasion. That day, I made vows to myself in front of my loved ones:

I promised to take myself in sickness and in health.

I promised to take myself for richer or for poorer.

I promised to love and cherish myself.

I promised to maintain perspective about what true problems are.

Most of all, I promised to keep the reserve off my life.

I had realized that you can't turn to others to complete yourself; only you can complete yourself. Only when you fully recognize that you are the one putting a reserve on your life and limiting your happiness are you able to cast it off and open yourself up to the right business, parental, romantic, or other relationship.

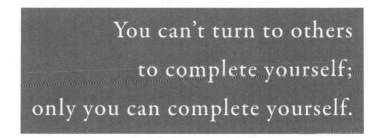

You can't turn to others to complete yourself; only you can complete yourself.

It was in that spirit that I vowed to prevent any internal or external situation from restricting the possibilities for my life. When facing any compromising situation, I committed to ask myself, "At what cost?"

At what cost to myself am I giving in to fear?

At what cost to myself am I keeping this bad habit?

At what cost to myself am I staying in this toxic relationship?

Yes, we will all fall down and find ourselves in pieces again. In fact, by the time you've read this, I'll probably have done the same. That's not the point. The point is, how do you handle the pain? Do you stay in misery, or do you use the pain to refashion yourself into a stronger, kinder, more generous person? Only you can choose. One path comes with a giant stop sign; the other will take you on a long and rewarding journey to fulfillment and impact.

Make the commitment to yourself always to accept yourself, challenge yourself, and protect your emotional, spiritual, and financial health. Whether you opt to commemorate it with a ceremony or not, you must find a way to be accountable to yourself. Life will knock us down more times than we care to think, which is why it is crucial to have some sort of safeguard in place to protect your vow to yourself to live life absolute.

After sharing about my self-marriage ceremony on social media, I was amazed to discover that so many women decided to do the same. Some had actual wedding rings made for the occasion; others did not. Some organized large parties; others held casual get-togethers in their house. The scope of the event had no impact on its import: these women—and men—were committing to taking control of their life by releasing it to self-love, empathy, optimism, and generosity of spirit.

Part of the significance of hosting an actual ceremony for this vow to self is the value added by your witnesses. At my self-wedding, my good friend Oscar De Las Salas with all sincerity asked me, "This is all well and good, Tish, but what can we do to help you keep this vow?"

Your witnesses should do what they would do for any couple whose wedding they have been a part of. If they knew the couple was fighting perpetually, or drinking too much, or flirting with other people, would they not feel compelled to sit the couple down and talk with them? The same goes for the person committing to live a no-reserve life: If their loved ones see them out of balance, with complete disregard for how their actions are impacting their soul, they need to bring it to their attention and help them honor the vows they made to their self.

Remember, your word is your value. And your word to yourself is the most important promise of all. If you don't keep your vows to yourself, you will not be able to keep them to other people. Add the greatest value to your life, and free yourself to receive the greatest rewards, by committing now to live with no limitations. Solidify your word with some physical symbol of that promise to always pick up the pieces and become a stronger, better version of yourself. A bid beyond your wildest dreams awaits you, but only if you *live with no reserve.*

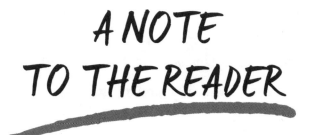

A NOTE
TO THE READER

There is one thing that I have learned regarding every single practice I have shared with you, and it's that none of them will get you the life of your dreams if you don't believe in yourself. So many people tell me that my belief in them enabled them to change their life, but as I explain in the chapter on mentorship, that's not really the case—it's their newfound belief in themselves after getting that external validation that creates the mental shift. The tools outlined in this book will help you ignite a belief in yourself, but you must ultimately light the flame. Not trusting yourself, not seeing your own value, is the biggest reserve you can possibly placc on your life. Recognize your worth—identify what you can give the world right now, as you are—and let that belief in yourself awaken your soul and set you free to live your best life. Blessings on your journey.

Letitia Frye

"Every moment spent in the wrong life is a moment not spent in the right one."

Join me on Instagram: @letitia_frye.

Share your stories of overcoming limitations using the hashtag #noreserve.

ABOUT THE AUTHOR

Currently celebrating over sixteen years in the auction business and having raised over $500 million dollars for charity, Letitia Frye has truly earned her title as America's foremost "auctiontainer." She is a beautiful, elegant, multi-talented, bilingual (English/Spanish) woman who is a big success in a field generally occupied by men. She has an innovative flair and treats each event as a "special" performance.

Letitia is able to effortlessly combine her expertise in entertainment, fashion, and fundraising and her humanitarian efforts to help so many in need and make a difference in people's lives. After a devastating accident in which she was struck by a car while running, leading to a traumatic brain injury, combined with the sudden death of the father of her children, Letitia decided to broaden her span beyond auctions in order to help more people. Ms. Frye is now a motivational speaker and author and believes that her passion for others is the secret to success in work and life.

Letitia has spent many years working with orphans in Haiti, volunteering for Doctors in Hospice, spending time with hospital researchers, rescuing abused and abandoned animals, volunteering at various camps for children, and granting wishes through the Make-A-Wish Foundation. She believes the only way to understand the mission of a charity or nonprofit is to personally provide time and effort to help those in need. As a formally trained actress with a degree in theater from The University of Southern California, Letitia literally dives into her work as an actor does to prepare for a role, immersing herself in every aspect of it so that she can better understand her client.

Letitia has received many awards for her work in the community, both locally and across the country. She received the prestigious Babe Caylor Leadership Award in 2017 for her work with LGBTQ youth. Letitia was a 2018 finalist for the ATHENA Award, an honor she holds so very near to her heart, as she has mentored over 60 men and women free of charge to help them better their lives, an enormous factor in being made an Athena. Her most humbling honors have come with having two of the awards she received being named after her: The 1N10 Letitia Frye Excellence in Fundraising Award and the St Jude Children's Research Hospital Letitia Frye Humanitarian Award.

Although she works all over the United States and outside of the country, Letitia calls Scottsdale, Arizona, her home. When not onstage, you can find her running through the beautiful scenery of North Scottsdale, mentoring a woman into her dream life, or on an adventure with her kids. Letitia has two beautiful children, whom she accounts for helping her tackle every obstacle that has come in front of her, and for her continued success in all fields of her career. You can learn more about Letitia at Letitiafrye.com, or follow Letitia on all of her adventures on Instagram @letitia_frye.

www.soundwisdom.com